MESSAGES OF GLORY

THE NARRATIVE ART OF ROMAN CATHOLICISM

MESSAGES OF GLORY

THE NARRATIVE ART OF ROMAN CATHOLICISM

photographs by ROBERT A. FLISCHEL, JOE SIMON *and* JAY YOCIS

preface by ANNE HUSTED BURLEIGH · *introduction by* REVEREND CHRISTOPHER ARMSTRONG
text by MONSIGNOR WILLIAM CLEVES *and* MARGO WARMINSKI

DAVID-FLISCHEL ENTERPRISES, LLC
CINCINNATI, OHIO

presented by

XAVIER UNIVERSITY

OUR LADY OF VICTORY AND PEACE

This sculpture of the Madonna by artist Ernest Bruce Haswell
was dedicated in July, 1943. *Carved in Bedford Limestone, this statue
is the centerpiece of a shrine honoring the Sons of Xavier who serve the armed
forces of our nation. Xavier University, Cincinnati, Oh.*

PUBLISHERS Robert A. Flischel & Kim David

EDITOR Robert A. Flischel

DESIGN Madison Design Group

MANAGING EDITOR Mara Mulvihill

PHOTOGRAPHERS Robert A. Flischel, Joe Simon & Jay Yocis

SENIOR EDITOR & RESEARCH DIRECTOR Margo Warminski

CHAPTER INTRODUCTORY ESSAYS & ECCLESIASTICAL ADVISOR
Monsignor William Cleves

INTRODUCTION Reverend Christopher Armstrong

PREFACE Anne Husted Burleigh

CONTRIBUTING EDITOR Emily Jolly

PRODUCTION COORDINATOR Lorena Gomez Mostajo

POST PRODUCTION ASSISTANTS Gavin Meyer, Suzi Jolly & Trevyn Riley

ADVISORY COMMITTEE Bill & Anne Burleigh, Tom McKiernan,
Scott David, Father Philip Seher, Conky Greiwe & Pat Gaito

DAVID-FLISCHEL ENTERPRISES, LLC

TELEPHONE (513) 272-2700
(513) 271-3113
EMAIL office@messagesofglory.com

Flischel, Robert A.
Messages of Glory, The Narrative Art of Roman Catholicism /
PUBLISHERS, Robert A. Flischel and Kim David; DESIGN,
Madison Design Group; MANAGING EDITOR, Mara Mulvihill;
PHOTOGRAPHERS, Robert A. Flischel, Joe Simon and Jay Yocis;
WRITERS, Margo Warminski, Monsignor William Cleves,
Father Christopher Armstrong and Anne Husted Burleigh

ISBN (hardcover) 0974596280
Library of Congress Control Number: 2011913714

front cover
St. Elizabeth of Hungary, photographed at The Vineyard Central
Community Church, (formerly old St. Elizabeth), Norwood, Oh.
Window by F.X. Zettler, Munich, Germany.

frontispiece
Carved wooden crucifixion scene, maker unknown,
framed by a Gothic stained glass window. C.J. Connick
Associates of Boston, Ma, in St. Mary Church, Hyde Park

dedication page
The Good Samaritan, maker unknown, St. Aloysius Church,
Elmwood Place, now Our Lady of Lavang Parish.

TABLE OF CONTENTS

PREFACE

BY ANNE HUSTED BURLEIGH

Our Christian life requires us to make a pilgrimage. To be a Christian is to be nothing less than a pilgrim, to receive a mission both universal in its purpose of union with God and particular in the unique way our mission is to be lived by each of us.

As everyone knows who prays the steps up to the Church of the Holy Cross-Immaculata on Mount Adams every Good Friday, the Christian life of pilgrimage has a beginning and an end — an end that we trust and pray will draw us further and deeper in love and knowledge of Christ, of ourselves, and of our neighbor. Like the Good Friday pilgrims climbing the steps, the Christian comes to understand that his unfolding pilgrimage through time and history is not only his undeniable vocation, but it is also his specifically gifted, unrepeatable path to an eternity that is beyond history. His alpha came at the moment of His conception. His omega will arrive only after He has toiled through time, with the Holy Spirit directing the providentially designated mission given especially to Him, when He will pass through death to eternal life to meet His Lord face to face.

It is our blessing that we do not make our pilgrimage alone. We travel from God, to God — and always with God and with other people. Even though a degree of loneliness is part of our condition since Adam and Eve disobeyed God in the garden, loneliness is deceptive. Our real way is with and through God and others — in communion with them.

Those who have come before us, whose wisdom gleaned from their own journeys laid the foundation and paved the way for our own, are as indispensable to our pilgrimage through life as the living souls who travel alongside us. We owe it to these forebears to hold them in memory. We owe them our remembering of the institutions, the artifacts, the traditions, the ways of being that they left to us. Those gifts are our inheritance, our spiritual and cultural trust. Our memory of our handed-down trust, our memory of what has been given to us, clarifies and illumines our present path.

St. Thomas Aquinas classified this gratitude we owe to God and to our parents and our country as a form of piety that is ultimately an extension of justice, one of the four cardinal virtues. Our debt to God who made us, to our parents through whom we were made, and to our Church and our country under whose protection we live, is a debt we cannot possibly repay. Our only proper response is gratitude and a willingness to pass on in turn to the next generation what we ourselves have received.

Those Catholics who have come before us here in the Ohio Valley have left to us in Greater Cincinnati an inestimable treasure of sacred art for which, as St. Thomas Aquinas would say, we cannot ever be adequately grateful. These exquisitely beautiful images in glass, paint, mosaic, and stone, images of all the scenes and stories of salvation history, are sometimes well-known to us who live and worship here, but often as not these images are mostly unknown and unsung. Yet the artists who with their minds, hearts, and hands created them clearly intended that we should be the recipients and beneficiaries of these reflections of God's loveliness.

Thanks to the keen artistic eye of Robert Flischel, who for twenty years has photographed these sacred works, the images are available at last to be viewed in *Messages of Glory: The Narrative Art of Roman Catholicism*.

May you receive this book as a means of prayer for your own pilgrimage, as a testament to the devotion of generations of Catholics who established these memorials, and as a repository of a priceless and irreplaceable collection of sacred art that reflects the richness of our Catholic culture.

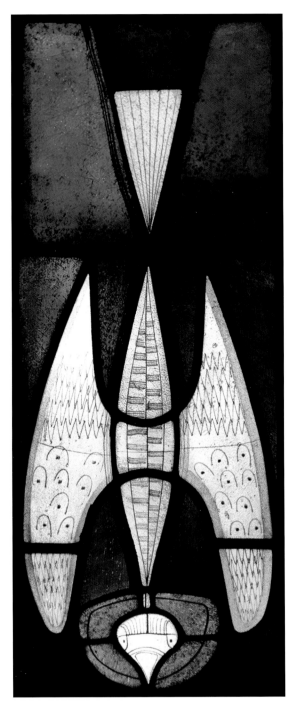

A series of contemporary stained glass panels from a
window wall celebrating the Creation. *Windows by Emil Frei
Stained Glass of St. Louis, Mo, in St. Gertrude Church, Madeira, Oh.*

IX

INTRODUCTION

BY REVEREND CHRISTOPHER ARMSTRONG

My first exposure to ecclesiastical art was in my parish church of St. Albert the Great, Kettering, Ohio. The building was divided between the "church-side," the original worship space, and the "chapel-side," a large addition built sometime in the 1950s. Thus there was no back wall to the sanctuary. The sanctuary itself was painted a dusty blue and decorated with white crosses. From the church side looking into the chapel side, on the lintel, were images taken from the book of Revelation. Later, I would learn that it was the Lamb of God, once slain, who lives forever. The lamb was resting on a book with seven seals. On either side of the lamb, in that narrow space, the planets of the universe whirled around. I was particularly taken with the rings of the planet Saturn. Still later I would learn that the decorator was Gerhard Lamers, a German-born muralist who was to decorate several churches throughout the Archdiocese of Cincinnati and the Midwest.

In the 1970s at the college seminary of St. Gregory the Great, I met Fr. Don Tenoever, teacher, mentor and eventually friend. Fr. Tenoever taught not only American Literature, but the History of Art and Architecture as well as the History of Music. It was in his classes that I caught not just what he taught but his own enthusiasm for high culture. For example, he illustrated his lectures with a vast collection of glass mounted slides. We shared his awe as he explained one beautiful painting or building after another. But more than that, he was an erudite practitioner. In particular, under Archbishop Alter, he was responsible for the renovation of the Cathedral of St. Peter in Chains in the late 1950s.

We had many wonderful discussions about that edifice as well as numerous "treasured churches" throughout the Archdiocese of Cincinnati. When he died in 1997, it was as if a library had burnt down, a building had collapsed or an old Master had been lost forever.

But for me, Fr. Tenoever's lasting legacy has been his influence on the cultural, historical and artistic life of the Archdiocese. In many ways, this present volume reflects that influence since it was Fr. Tenoever who brought Robert Flischel and me together the year before he died. I like to think that this book is a paraphrase of Christopher Wren's epitaph in the Cathedral of St. Paul in London: "If you seek his monument, look around you." This volume also illustrates a line from Pasternak's *Dr. Zhivago*, "Art has two constants, two unending concerns: it always meditates on death and thus creates life. All great, genuine art resembles and continues the Revelation of St. John."

opposite page
A collection of artisan's signatures and maker's marks discovered during the creation of this book.

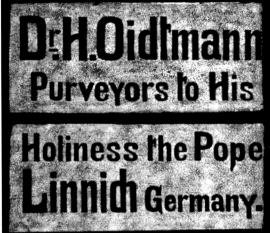

Chapter I

ANGELS

GUARDIAN ANGEL

A disabled man is rescued by a rainbow-winged guardian angel from a sea creature.
A rich Neoclassical frame surrounds the image. *Window by F.X. Zettler of Munich, Germany,*
in old St. Paul's Church, Over-the-Rhine (now Verdin Museum / Bell Event Center).

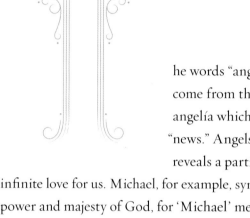

The words "angel" and "evangelization" come from the same Greek word — angelía which means "message" or "news." Angels are messengers; each reveals a particular aspect of God's infinite love for us. Michael, for example, symbolizes the overwhelming power and majesty of God, for 'Michael' means "Who is like God?" Raphael is a sign of God's healing, for 'Raphael' means "God heals." 'Gabriel' means "God is strong," and represents God's help in those times when we know that mere human strength cannot succeed. It is entirely fitting, therefore, that Michael is the angel who is victorious over God's enemies (see Daniel 10:12; Revelation 12:7; Jude 1:9). It is Raphael through whom Tobit is healed of his blindness (see Tobit 11:7–15; 12:15–20), and Gabriel who answers the question of the Virgin Mary: "How can this be...?" (see Luke 1:26–38).

The idea of the presence of guardian angels in our lives, while not a defined article of faith, is held by such notable Catholic thinkers as Saint Jerome, Saint John Chrysostom, Saint Basil, and Saint Thomas Aquinas. Some see a reference to guardian angels in Exodus 32:34, where God said to Moses, "See, my angel will go before you," and in Psalm 91:11, where "God commands the angels to guard you in all your ways."

AGONY IN THE GARDEN

Following the Last Supper, Jesus prays in Gethsemane before his arrest. After an agonizing struggle, God sends an angel to comfort him.
Window by F.X. Zettler of Munich, Germany, in St. Mark Church, Evanston.

18

GABRIEL

above
St. Gabriel raises a trumpet in an arched
paneled window. *Window by Emil Frei
Stained Glass of St. Louis, Mo, in St. Ursula
Academy Chapel, East Walnut Hills.*

below
Symbols of Gabriel: a horn and lily. *Detail
of window by Riordan Art Glass, Middletown,
Oh, in St. Andrew Church, Milford, Oh.*

right
*Window by Franz Mayer of Munich, Germany,
in St. Boniface Church, Northside.*

RAPHAEL

above
Raphael, bearing a scepter.
*Window by F.X. Zettler of Munich,
Germany, in the Provincial House
Chapel of the Sisters of Notre Dame,
Park Hills, Ky.*

left
Raphael bearing a fish, symbol
of the Eucharist. *Window by
Franz Mayer of Munich, Germany,
in St. Andrew Church, Avondale.*

THE ANGELS
OF CINCINNATI

Two exquisite white marble angels stand in postures of prayer and adoration: arms crossed, hands folded. Created by Odoardo Fantacchioti in the late 1840s, the angels were among the first European sculptures brought to Cincinnati. Their first home in Cincinnati was St. Peter in Chains Cathedral. During the renovation of the Cathedral in the 1950s, these sculptures did not fit the design scheme and were ordered to be chopped up and thrown in a dump. However, Monsignor William J. Anthony stepped in and rescued this art, moving them to his parish, St. Teresa of Avila, in West Price Hill. They were displayed in the old St. Teresa until a new church was built in the 1960s.

When the new church opened, they again failed to match the design and were moved behind a curtain in the bingo hall. Two art historians, Ted Gantz and Liz Schuer discovered them during an art inventory commissioned by the Archdiocese in the late 1990s. Their importance became clear and Father Larry Tharp, pastor of St. Teresa, made a commitment to save and restore them.

The conclusion of this saga occurred when the late Suzanne Warrington came forward and underwrote their restoration. They are now on loan to the Cincinnati Art Museum and can be seen in the Cincinnati Wing.

20

right
Adoring angel.

opposite page
Prayerful angel.

Prayerful angels gaze
down upon Jewish and
Christian worship services.
Aaron prefigures the
sacrifice of Jesus: His
sacrifice is commemorated
sacramentally today.

23

Murals by Frank Duveneck
in Cathedral Basilica of the
Assumption, Covington, Ky.

24

Graceful angels' wing of
white carrara marble. *This
statue stands under the coffered
half-dome of St. Ursula Academy
Chapel, East Walnut Hills.*

GUARDIAN ANGELS

above
An angel guides a little girl,
her eyes lifted to heaven.
*Detail of window, maker
unknown, in St. Agnes Church,
Fort Wright, Ky.*

right
Swagged garlands
and a border of acanthus
leaves frame a watchful
angel. *Window, maker
unknown, in St. Aloysius
Church, Elmwood Place, Oh
(now Our Lady of Lavang Parish).*

THE·GIFT·OF
BARBARA·SANGER

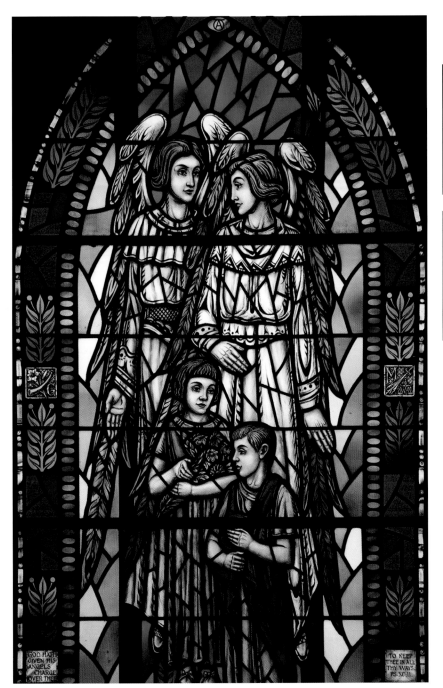

above
"God hath given his angels
charge over thee / To keep
thee in all thy ways"
(Psalm 90:11). *Details of
window by Riordan Art Glass,
Middletown, Oh, in St. Andrew
Church, Milford, Oh.*

left
Two protective angels guard
a young boy and girl. *The
lancet-arched window by Riordan
Art Glass, Middletown, Oh, in
St. Andrew Church, Milford, Oh.*

28

opposite page
Heavenly light shines down upon St. John the Baptist and the
young Jesus, garbed in red and purple. *Window by Emil Frei Stained
Glass of St. Louis, Mo, in St. Ursula Academy Chapel, East Walnut Hills.*

above
"Blessed are the dead who die in the Lord." A righteous life
is the doorway to eternal life. *Windows by Franz Mayer of Munich,
Germany, in Cathedral Basilica of the Assumption, Covington, Ky.*

above & below
These painted icons, lavished
with gold, are part of the
original altar in St. Mary
Church, Hyde Park.

opposite page
A serene angel in brilliant
sunlight, sculpted from white
carrara marble. *Immaculate
Heart of Mary Chapel, The Summit
Country Day School, Hyde Park.*

Chapter II

A "LITANY" OF SAINTS

It has been reported that Sir Isaac Newton, when he was congratulated for seeing further into the mysteries of the universe than anybody, replied that if it were true that he had seen further, it was only because he found himself standing on the shoulders of giants. The saints are the giants on whose shoulders we stand. Their example reminds us that we share their vocation, namely, that we are ourselves called to be giants on whose shoulders our descendants stand. Thus it is that the Church, the Body of Christ, is built from living stones (see 1 Peter 2:5) into a temple of God's glory.

When we wish to learn to do something well, we turn to the great ones. It does not matter in which field we aspire to excellence; whatever our chosen field, we always seek inspiration from the giants. The Church's veneration of saints, then, has a solid human foundation. In honoring the saints and seeking to imitate them, we do what is natural for humans to do; we turn to the "experts." Thus, in Catholic spirituality, there rose the tradition of patron saints, those to whom we turn for intercession and guidance in the varied vocations that we have received from God.

SAINT ELIZABETH

St. Elizabeth of Hungary (1207–1231), devoted
her adult life to caring for the poor and suffering.
This window depicts Elizabeth and her four children
being evicted from the palace after the death
of her husband. *Window by F.X. Zettler of Munich,
Germany, in old St. Elizabeth Church, Norwood, Oh
(now Vineyard Central Community Church).*

SAINT LOUIS

St. Louis (1223–1267) is one of the patron saints of the
Secular Franciscan Order. As king of France, his reign
brought peace, justice and important civil reforms.
Here he is depicted in a fleur-de-lis robe, with scepter

SAINT BIBIANA

Bibiana was a Roman virgin and martyr of the fourth
century A.D. A basilica was named in her honor,
supposedly by Pope Simplicius, which still stands.
Bibiana is the patron saint against earthquakes

TRIO OF SAINTS

Created by Franz Mayer of Munich,
Germany, these windows are in the style
of the original 12th century stained glass
of Augsburg Cathedral in Germany.

St. Teresa of Avila Church, West Price Hill.

SAINT DOMINIC

Shown in his characteristic preaching stance, St. Dominic
(1170–1221) was the founder of the Order of Preachers, or
Dominican Order. His motto is "to praise, to bless, to preach." He
is the patron saint of astronomers and the Dominican Republic.

St. Angela instructs a group of five
girls in the spiritual life (prayer)
and the domestic arts (sewing).
*Window by C.J. Connick Associates
of Boston, Ma, in the former Ursuline
Academy Chapel, Walnut Hills.*

SAINT ANGELA MERICI

St. Angela Merici (1474–1540) was the founder of the Ursuline Order. Devoted
solely to teaching young girls, it was the first teaching order established in the Church.
Here Angela teaches the alphabet to an eager young learner. *Window maker unknown,
Sacred Heart Chapel, Ursulines of Brown County, Oh.*

SAINT JULIE BILLIART

St. Julie Billiart (1751–1816) founded the Congregation of the Sisters of Notre Dame de Namur,
a teaching order devoted to the education of young girls and training of religious teachers.
During her remarkable life she spent 22 years as a bedridden paralytic, gathering followers
around her bedside. *Window rescued from the former St. Joseph Academy in Columbus, Oh, now resides
in the Sisters of Notre Dame de Namur Health Center, Reading, Oh.*

SAINT LAWRENCE

opposite page

The martyring of St. Lawrence in Rome, 258 A.D. *Window by*
Emil Frei Stained Glass of St. Louis, Mo, in St. Lawrence Church, Price Hill.

SAINT GEORGE

above

A brilliantly painted triptych depicts St. George, a martyr who became the patron
saint of England, Germany, Portugal, the Boy Scouts and soldiers. *Formerly in St. George*
Monastery, Clifton Heights, now in St. Monica-St. George Church, Fairview Heights.

SAINT PATRICK

right

St. Patrick, crosier in
hand, points to the snakes
slithering away from Ireland.
*Mosaic by Vatican Studios, in
St. Gregory the Great Chapel,
Mount Washington.*

opposite page

The Church's patron holds
in outstretched hand the
dainty shamrock of his
adopted land. The wooden
statue is painted and gilded.
St. Patrick Church, Maysville, Ky.

IRISH BLESSING

May the road rise to meet you,
May the wind be always at your back.
May the sun shine warm upon your face,
The rains fall soft upon your fields.
And until we meet again,
May God hold you in the palm of His hand.

May God be with you and bless you:
May you see your children's children.
May you be poor in misfortune,
Rich in blessings.
May you know nothing but happiness
From this day forward.

May the road rise up to meet you
May the wind be always at your back
May the warm rays of sun fall upon your home
And may the hand of a friend always be near.

May green be the grass you walk on,
May blue be the skies above you,
May pure be the joys that surround you,
May true be the hearts that love you.

SAINT CECILIA

"St. Cecilia, pray for us."
This intricate lunette
portrays Cecilia, martyr
and patron saint of music,
with a host of angels singing
praise to God. St. Gregory
and King David represent
Christian and Jewish
musical traditions. The
surrounding medallions
depict lutes, harps,
trumpets and organ pipes.
*Window by Oidtmann Studios of
Linnich, Germany, in St. Martin
of Tours Church, Cheviot, Oh.*

SAINT MARGARET OF ANTIOCH

Bearing a cross and palm,
she stands amid a sunset
scene in an exquisite
Renaissance arch. *Window
by Emil Frei Stained Glass of St.
Louis, Mo, in St. Ursula Academy
Chapel, East Walnut Hills.*

ST. MARGARET.

IN MEMORY OF MARGARET DUER HENRY AND FAMILY.

47

SAINT URSULA

According to legend, Ursula
was a British Christian saint
who was murdered, along with
her attendants, in Germany
en route to a pilgrimage.
*Window by Emil Frei Stained
Glass of St. Louis, Mo, in St. Ursula
Academy Chapel, East Walnut Hills.*

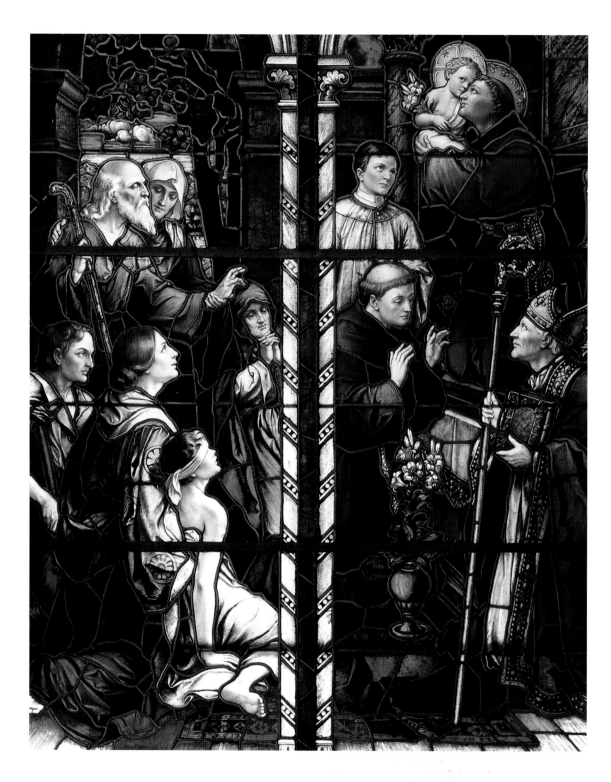

48

SAINT ANTHONY

Scenes from the life of St. Anthony of Padua (c. 1195–1231),
a Franciscan priest and brilliant preacher of the Incarnate
Word. *Diptych window, by Franz Mayer of Munich, Germany,
in old St. George Church, Clifton Heights.*

Lord, make me an instrument of your peace.
Where there is hatred, let me sow love;
where there is injury, pardon;
where there is doubt, faith;
where there is despair, hope;
where there is darkness, light;
and where there is sadness, joy.

O Divine Master,
grant that I may not so much seek
to be consoled as to console;
to be understood as to understand;
to be loved as to love.
For it is in giving that we receive;
it is in pardoning that we are pardoned;
and it is in dying that we are born to eternal life.

Amen.

49

SAINT FRANCIS OF ASSISI

Founder of the Franciscan Order, Francis (c. 1181–1226)
is the patron saint of Italy, merchants, animals and ecology.
*A contemporary mosaic, abstracted and powerful, by Peter Recker,
Rome, Italy, in St. Clare Convent Chapel, Hartwell.*

I CORINTHIANS 13:1—7

If I speak in human and angelic tongues, but do not have love,
I am a resounding gong or a clashing cymbal.

And if I have the gift of prophecy, and comprehend all mysteries
and all knowledge; if I have all faith so as to move mountains,
but do not have love, I am nothing.

If I give away everything I own, and if I hand my body over
so that I may boast, but do not have love, I gain nothing.

Love is patient, love is kind. It is not jealous, (love) is not pompous,
it is not inflated, it is not rude, it does not seek its own interests,
it is not quick-tempered, it does not brood over injury,
it does not rejoice over wrongdoing but rejoices with the truth.
It bears all things, believes all things, hopes all things, endures all things.

SAINT PAUL

above

St. Paul is known as the Apostle to the Gentiles. *Neo-Gothic window
by C.J. Connick Associates of Boston, Ma, in St. Mary Church, Hyde Park.*

opposite page

En route to persecute Christians in Damascus, Paul is blinded
by a vision of Jesus. *Window by F.X. Zettler, Munich, Germany, in old
St. Paul's Church, Over-the-Rhine (now Verdin Museum / Bell Event Center).*

Chapter III

THE BEATITUDES

BLESSED ARE THE CLEAN OF HEART, FOR THEY WILL SEE GOD

Garbed in flowing gowns and wreathed with flowers, women and children walk bearing lilies,
a symbol of purity. *Window by Tyrol Art Glass Company of Innsbruck, Austria, in St. Catharine Church, Westwood.*

Blessed are the clean of heart: for they shall see God

The word 'beatitude' refers to a literary form that appears in the Old and New Testaments. A beatitude (from the Latin 'beatus' which means "happy" or "blessed") is a proclamation that someone is blessed because of a certain virtue or because of divine favor. The Book of Psalms, for example, begins with a beatitude: "Happy those who do not follow the counsel of the wicked, nor go in the way of sinners, nor sit in company with scoffers." Other instances can be found in The Book of Proverbs 8:33 —"Happy the man who obeys me and happy those who keep my ways…" and the book of the prophet Isaiah 32:20 —"Happy are you who sow beside every stream…"

Of course, when Christians think of the beatitudes they usually think of the beatitudes in Matthew's Gospel (see Matthew 5:3–12) or those in the Gospel of Luke (see Luke 6:20–23). The striking feature of both of these sets of beatitudes is the challenge they present; they come from one who does not look on life with human wisdom only. We are not accustomed, after all, to think of suffering, mourning, and persecution as blessings. The beatitudes proclaim the wisdom of God, whose thoughts and ways are high above ours, just as the heavens are high above the earth (see Isaiah 55:9).

BLESSED ARE THE POOR IN SPIRIT,
FOR THEIRS IS THE KINGDOM OF HEAVEN

An angel brings the glad tidings of Christ's birth to lowly shepherds, attended by a heavenly host. *Window by Oidtmann Studios of Linnich, Germany, in St. Martin of Tours Church, Cheviot, Oh.*

BLESSED ARE THE POOR IN SPIRIT

SERMON ON THE MOUNT

MATTHEW 5:1-10

When He saw the crowds, He went up the
mountain, and after He had sat down, His disciples
came to Him. He began to teach them, saying:

Blessed are the poor in spirit,
for theirs is the kingdom of heaven.

Blessed are they who mourn,
for they will be comforted.

Blessed are the meek,
for they will inherit the land.

Blessed are they who hunger and thirst
for righteousness, for they will be satisfied.

Blessed are the merciful,
for they will be shown mercy.

Blessed are the clean of heart,
for they will see God.

Blessed are the peacemakers,
for they will be called children of God.

Blessed are they who are persecuted for the sake of
righteousness, for theirs is the kingdom of heaven.

Blessed are you when they insult you and persecute
you and utter every kind of evil against you (falsely)
because of me.

Rejoice and be glad, for your reward
will be great in heaven.

56

The Sermon on the Mount is recounted in all four Gospels. Jesus taught by word and deed,
and His teachings on the Mount — the Beatitudes — outline the Christian path to happiness.
Leon Lippert mural in Sacred Heart Church, Bellevue, Ky (now Divine Mercy Parish).

BLESSED ARE THEY WHO MOURN,
FOR THEY WILL BE COMFORTED

Jesus comforts a dying man, taking his hand as mourners weep and gather around the bedside.
Window by Oidtmann Studios of Linnich, Germany, in St. Martin of Tours Church, Cheviot, Oh.

BLESSED ARE THE MEEK,
FOR THEY WILL INHERIT THE LAND

The Woman at the Well. Resting at a well, St. Peter at His side, Jesus encounters a Samaritan
woman drawing water. He asks her for a drink and speaks to her of God's "living water."
Window by Oidtmann Studios of Linnich, Germany, in St. Martin of Tours Church, Cheviot, Oh.

BLESSED ARE THOSE
WHO HUNGER AND
THIRST FOR
RIGHTEOUSNESS,
FOR THEY WILL
BE SATISFIED

right
Double lancet window by Tyrol
Art Glass Company of Innsbruck,
Austria, in St. Catharine Church,
Westwood.

BLESSED ARE
THE MERCIFUL,
FOR THEY WILL
BE SHOWN MERCY

opposite page
The story of the Good
Samaritan: "Love your
neighbor as yourself." *Window*
by Oidtmann Studios of Linnich,
Germany, in St. John the Evangelist
Church of Covington, Ky.

BLESSED ARE THE MERCIFUL

BLESSED ARE THE CLEAN OF HEART, FOR THEY WILL SEE GOD

Followers, men, women and children, cluster around Jesus and kneel at His feet. *Window by Oidtmann Studios of Linnich, Germany, in St. John the Evangelist Church, Covington, Ky.*

63

BLESSED ARE
THE PEACEMAKERS,
FOR THEY WILL BE
CALLED CHILDREN
OF GOD

Double lancet window by Tyrol Art Glass Company of Innsbruck, Austria, in St. Catharine Church, Westwood.

BLESSED ARE THEY WHO ARE PERSECUTED FOR THE SAKE OF
RIGHTEOUSNESS, FOR THEIRS IS THE KINGDOM OF HEAVEN.

St. Thomas Becket. "Who will rid me of this troublesome priest?" Archbishop of Canterbury
during the reign of Henry II, St. Thomas Becket (1118–1170) spoke truth to power and lost his
life as a result. *Two panels by Tyrol Art Glass Company of Innsbruck, Austria, St. Catharine Church, Westwood.*

64

BLESSED ARE THEY | THAT SUFFER PERSECUTION FOR | JUSTICE'SAKE

BLESSED ARE THEY | THAT SUFFER PERSECU | TION FOR JUSTICE'S AKE

above
Jesus is made to carry His
cross. *Window by Oidtmann
Studios of Linnich, Germany,
in St. Martin of Tours Church,
Cheviot, Oh.*

below
St. Stephen (d. c. 36 A.D.)
was the first martyr, whose
death is recorded in the
Acts of the Apostles (Acts
7:55 – 60b). He was arrested
on charges of blasphemy
and stoned to death by
the Sanhedrin. *Window by
Oidtmann Studios of Linnich,
Germany, in St. John the Evangelist
Church, Covington, Ky.*

65

Chapter IV

THE SACRAMENTS

PRESENTED BY THE
ST JOSEPH'S MENS
SOCIETY.

acramentum' was the Latin translation of the Greek 'mysterion' (mystery). The seven sacraments are ways in which the faithful share in the mystery of God's healing and saving love. Saint Thomas Aquinas said that sacraments are given to us at all the important times of our lives. Traditionally, the sacraments have been classified into three kinds.

The Sacraments of Christian Initiation (Baptism, Confirmation, Eucharist) provide the basis of our life in Christ. Through Baptism we are "immersed" into the mysteries of salvation. Through Confirmation, baptismal grace is confirmed, that is, brought to completion. In the Eucharist, our Christian initiation is completed, and we are given a foretaste of the heavenly banquet.

In the Sacraments of Healing (Anointing of the Sick and the Sacrament of Penance and Reconciliation) Jesus continues His ministry of healing and salvation. Sickness and sin are still part of life on earth; these sacraments show the victory of Jesus over the forces of sin and death.

The Sacraments at the Service of Communion (Marriage and Holy Orders) give those who receive them special graces to serve others. Through Marriage, a man and a woman become one flesh, and are called to be open to the begetting and raising of children. Through Holy Orders, men are called to exercise in the Church the mission that Jesus gave to the apostles. There are three degrees of this sacrament: deacon, priest, and bishop.

BAPTISM

John the Baptist baptizes Jesus in the Jordan River.
Window maker unknown, in St. Gabriel Church, Glendale, Oh.

EUCHARIST

above
A jewel-like trefoil cross and golden chalice.
*Detail of window by Larschied-Van Treeck of Milwaukee, Wi,
and Munich, Germany, in St. Cecilia Church, Oakley.*

opposite page
A First Communion Scene. *Window by F.X. Zettler,
Munich, Germany, formerly in St. Pius X Church, South
Cumminsville. This window was restored in 2011 to be
placed in St. Frances de Sales Church, Lebanon, Oh.*

EGO TE ABSOLVO

A PECCATIS TUIS

ACT OF CONTRITION

O my God,
I am heartily sorry for
having offended Thee,
and I detest all my sins,
because I dread the loss of heaven,
and the pains of hell;
but most of all because
they offend Thee, my God,
Who are all good and
deserving of all my love.
I firmly resolve,
with the help of Thy grace,
to confess my sins,
to do penance,
and to amend my life.

Amen.

73

PENANCE

opposite page
The act of confession. *Carved limestone relief
by sculptors Koepnick & Driesbach, façade
of St. Teresa of Avila Church, West Price Hill.*

above
"Ego te absolvo, A peccatis tuis:" "Therefore,
I absolve you from your sins." St. Vincent de Paul
grants absolution. *Detail of window by Riordan Art Glass,
Middletown, Oh, in St. Andrew Church, Milford, Oh.*

CONFIRMATION

opposite page

This window celebrates the feast of Pentecost and symbolizes the sacrament of Confirmation.
Window by Franz Mayer of Munich, Germany, Cathedral Basilica of the Assumption, Covington, Ky.

MARRIAGE

above

Set in an intricate Roman-arched diptych, a kneeling couple join hands
while the priest witnesses their exchange of promises. *Window by Franz Mayer
of Munich, Germany, in old St. George Church, Clifton Heights.*

HOLY ORDERS

above

A candidate for the priesthood is ordained. *Window by Franz Mayer of
Munich, Germany, in the Cathedral Basilica of the Assumption, Covington, Ky.*

ANOINTING OF THE SICK

opposite page

A priest anoints a dying woman for forgiveness of sin in final
preparation for heaven. *Window by Franz Mayer of Munich, Germany,
in the Cathedral Basilica of the Assumption, Covington, Ky.*

Chapter V

SYMBOLS AND ICONS

THE DOVE

Traditional Christian symbol of peace: a dove and olive branch.
Mosaic in old St. Paul's Church, Over-the-Rhine (now Verdin Museum / Bell Event Center).

'Synballo' is an ancient Greek verb that means "I meet." The literal meaning is "I throw together," and so the noun 'symbolon' came to mean a "token" or "outward sign." Saint Cyprian, in the middle of the third century, used this word to refer to what we now call the Apostles Creed, since the recitation of the Creed is an outward sign of that which we hold in our hearts.

'Eikon' is the Greek word for "likeness." Icons present to us a likeness of God or the saints.

There is a story told about Pope John XXIII, that he wrote the Latin phrase "non sumus angeli" (we are not angels) on a set of blueprints sent to him for his approval. When the architect received the blueprints, he could not understand what the pope meant. He asked some Vatican officials, who themselves did not understand the meaning of the phrase. At last the pope himself was asked. He said in reply that he wrote the phrase to remind the architect to include bathrooms in the building.

Because we are not angels, we need symbols and icons. Aristotle claimed, and Saint Thomas Aquinas agreed, that there is nothing in our minds that is not first in our senses. Symbols and icons (like sacraments and sacramentals) are necessary for us; they invite our attention only to point beyond themselves to even greater realities.

THE ROOSTER

A snowy rooster against a ruby roundel. The surrounding arch is shaded gold and green. *Window by Emil Frei Stained Glass of St. Louis, Mo, in Holy Family Church, Price Hill.*

THE ROOSTER

The rooster is traditionally a symbol of watchfulness
and vigilance because it rises early in the morning.

top left
Strutting rooster in relief. *St. William Church, West Price Hill.*

top center
Crowing rooster. *Mosaic in St. Dominic Church, Delhi Township, Oh.*

top right
Boldly stylized rooster. *Window by T. C. Esser Company of
Milwaukee Wi, in the old Jesuit Novitiate Chapel, Milford, Oh.*

bottom
Brilliantly colored rooster. *Detail of window by
Riordan Art Glass, Middletown, Oh, in old St. Elizabeth Church,
Norwood, Oh (now Vineyard Central Community Church).*

CROSSED KEYS

According to Christian tradition, Jesus handed
St. Peter the keys of heaven: a symbol of his new
authority (Matthew 16:19–20).

top right
Mosaic in St. William Church, West Price Hill.

bottom right
Detail of Gothic-style window by Franz Mayer of Munich,
Germany, in Immaculate Conception Chapel, Motherhouse
of the Sisters of Charity, Delhi Township, Oh.

ANGELS AND DEVILS

Devils tempt humanity to sin, but the power of God is stronger still.

top left
Shrieking winged devil. *Detail of window by Emil Frei Stained Glass of St. Louis, Mo, in St. Ursula Academy Chapel, East Walnut Hills.*

top right
Mary crushes the devil beneath her feet. *Detail of window by Franz Mayer of Munich, Germany, Cathedral Basilica of the Assumption, Covington, Ky.*

bottom
The devil tempts Jesus as he fasts and prays in the Judean desert for forty days and nights. *Detail of window by T.C. Esser Company of Milwaukee, Wi, in the old Jesuit Novitiate Chapel, Milford, Oh.*

opposite page
St. Michael vanquishes the devil. *Window by Radiant Arts Studio, Beach City, Oh, in All Saints Church, Walton, Ky.*

84

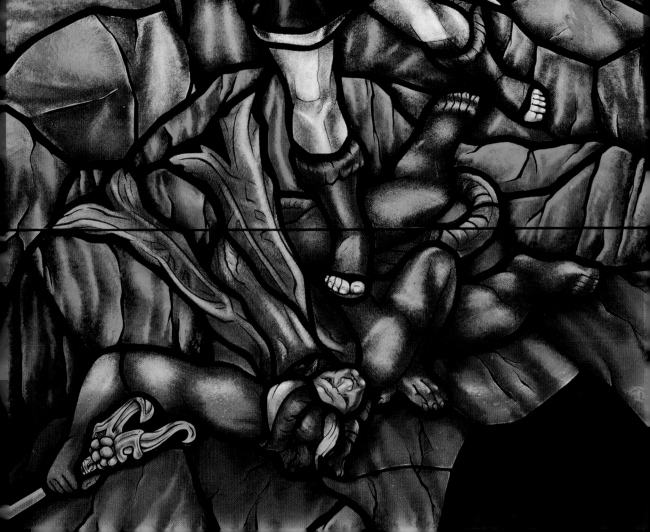

THE LAMB OF GOD

Jesus, the Lamb of God who takes away the sins of the world: part of the Communion rite.

top
Lamb on pilgrimage. *Detail of window by F.X. Zettler*
of Munich, Germany, in Mount St. Mary Seminary Chapel,
Norwood, Oh (now Our Lady of the Holy Spirit Center).

left
Beaded quatrefoil. *Detail of window by*
Larschied-Van Treeck, Milwaukee, Wi, and
Munich, Germany, in St. Cecilia Church, Oakley.

center left
Mosaic in St. Boniface Church, Northside.

center right
Roundel in St. Mary Church, Bethel, Oh. Formerly in
St. Michael the Archangel Church, Lower Price Hill.

right
Detail of window by Riordan Art Glass, Middletown,
Oh, in St. Andrew Church, Milford, Oh.

THE WHEAT AND GRAPES

Wheat and grapes, made into bread and wine, symbolize the body and blood of Christ in the Eucharist.

top left
Triple sheaf of wheat. Beaded octagon.
*Detail of a window by Franz Mayer of Munich,
Germany, in St. Boniface Church, Northside.*

top right
Grapes on the vine. Beaded hexagon.
*Detail of a window by Franz Mayer of Munich,
Germany, in St. Boniface Church, Northside.*

left & right
Tied sheaf of wheat and bunch of grapes.
*Detail of a window by Riordan Art Glass of
Middletown, Oh, in St. Andrew Church, Milford, Oh.*

center
Detail of a marble altar. *Mount
St. Mary Seminary Chapel, Norwood, Oh
(now Our Lady of the Holy Spirit Center).*

THE BUTTERFLY

The butterfly is a symbol of transformation
because of the process of metamorphosis.

above
Stylized butterfly. *Detail of window by Conrad Schmitt Studios
of New Berlin, Wi, in St. Clare Convent Chapel, Hartwell.*

below
Impressionistic butterfly. *Detail of window by Riordan Art Glass,
Middletown, Oh, in St. William Church, West Price Hill.*

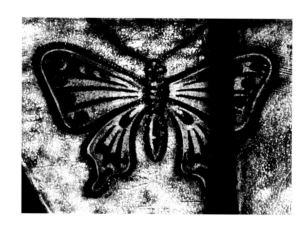

THE PEACOCK

To early Christians, peacocks symbolized immortality and eternal life because they believed the birds' flesh did not decay after death, and because they replace their feathers annually.

Peacock with magnificent plumage, in the brilliant shadow of a stained glass window. *Metal screen, St. William Church, West Price Hill.*

THE DOVE

The dove is a symbol of the soul and of the Holy Spirit,
signifying peace, gentleness and purity.

above
A dove peers through a
porthole window, suggesting
the story of Noah's ark. *Detail
of window, maker unknown, in St.
Clare Convent Chapel, Hartwell.*

top left
A night-flying dove, bearing
an olive branch. The anchor
symbolizes being rooted in
hope and faith. *Detail of window*

*by F.X. Zettler of Munich, Germany,
Mount St. Mary Seminary Chapel,
Norwood, Oh (now Our Lady of
the Holy Spirit Center).*

top right
Detail of a mural by
Gerhard Lamers, symbolizing
the Holy Spirit. *Holy Family
Church, Price Hill.*

center
Dove with olive branch and
eight-pointed star. *Wooden
plaque in Blessed Sacrament
Church, Ft. Mitchell, Ky.*

bottom left
Perching dove with olive
branch. *Limestone relief by
sculptors Koepnick & Driesbach
in St. Teresa of Avila Church,
West Price Hill.*

bottom right
Dove in flight with olive
sprig. *Detail of window by
T.C. Esser of Milwaukee, Wi,
in Our Lord Christ the King
Church, Mount Lookout.*

THE PASSION FLOWER

Parts of the plant have acquired meanings associated with Jesus' crucifixion. *Detail of window by Oidtmann Studios of Linnich, Germany, in St. John the Evangelist Church, Covington, Ky.*

THE SUNFLOWER

The sunflower turns its face to the sun, symbolizing adoration. *Detail of window (maker unknown) in St. Aloysius Church, Elmwood Place, Oh (now Our Lady of Lavang Parish).*

CONSIDER THE LILIES

LUKE 12:27–28

Or take the lilies: they do not spin, they
do not weave; but I tell you, Solomon in all his
splendor was not arrayed like any one of them.
If God clothes in such splendor the grass of
the field, which grows today and is thrown
on the fire tomorrow, how much more will
He provide for you, O weak in faith!

93

THE LILY

The lily is a symbol of purity and an emblem
of the Virgin Mary. The lily also has associations
with other saints, including St. Anthony of Padua.

opposite page
A pink-winged cherub in a gauzy cloud plucks
a lily. *Detail of window by Emil Frei Stained Glass of
St. Louis, Mo, in St. Lawrence Church, Price Hill.*

left
*Twining, Art Nouveau lilies, stained glass panel,
maker unknown, in St. Patrick Church, Maysville, Ky.*

THE TREES

In Jewish and Christian tradition, the olive is a symbol
of peace. It also signifies wisdom, fertility and abundance.

above left
Fruiting olive tree against
a starry sky. *Detail of window by
F.X. Zettler of Munich, Germany,
in Mount St. Mary Seminary
Chapel, Norwood, Oh (now Our
Lady of the Holy Spirit Center).*

below
"Truth will spring from the
earth; justice will look down
from heaven" (Psalm 85:12).
*Detail of window by Riordan Art
Glass, Middletown, in Blessed
Sacrament Church, Ft. Mitchell, Ky.*

above right
Olive tree bearing fruit.
*Detail of window by T.C. Esser of
Milwaukee, Wi, in the old Jesuit
Novitiate Chapel, Milford, Oh.*

THE
OMNISCIENT EYE

The Omniscient Eye of
God. Contained within
an equilateral triangle with
emanating rays, the all-seeing
eye, associated with the
Trinity, symbolizes the
omnipresence and
omniscience of God.

above
Detail of window, maker
unknown, in the St. Clare
Convent Chapel, Hartwell.

left
Detail of window by Franz
Mayer of Munich, Germany,
Cathedral Basilica of the
Assumption, Covington, Ky.

95

This series of eight windows features roundels
against a background of twining acanthus leaves.
The images were inspired by St. Francis of Assisi's
"Canticle of Brother Sun," which sings in simple
words of praise the glory and goodness of God.
The windows were created by C.J. Connick
Associates of Boston, Ma, the leading exponents
of the Neo-Gothic stained glass style in America.
The rich cool blues are a Connick hallmark:
they symbolize wisdom and heaven and recall
the colors of medieval glass.

*Details of windows in the Chapel of the Sacred Heart,
St. Anne's Convent, Melbourne, Ky.*

THE FISH

In Christianity, the fish is a symbol of abundance
and faith, particularly in the Gospel story of the
multiplication of loaves and fishes.

above
Brass relief, entrance façade of
St. Gertrude Church, Madeira, Oh.

below
IXOYE is an abbreviation in Greek letters
of "Jesus Christ, Son of God, Savior."
Carved limestone relief by Koepnick & Driesbach
in St. Teresa of Avila Church, West Price Hill.

right
Window by Emil Frei Stained Glass of St. Louis, Mo,
in St. Gertrude Church, Madeira, Oh.

THE SHIP

The ship has been a symbol of the Church
since the early days of Christianity.

above
Ship with trident mast, amphorae
and dove. *Wooden plaque in Blessed
Sacrament Church, Fort Mitchell, Ky.*

top left
Ship with billowing sail and Latin cross.
*Detail of window by C.J. Connick Associates
of Boston, Ma, in St. Mary Church, Hyde Park.*

bottom left
*Detail of a mural by Gerhard Lamers,
Church of the Annunciation, Clifton.*

THE TEN COMMANDMENTS

top left
Moses and the Ten
Commandments. *Detail
of window by C.J. Connick
Associates of Boston, Ma, in
St. Mary Church, Hyde Park.*

top right
*Detail of window by Franz Mayer
of Munich, Germany, in the
Cathedral Basilica of the
Assumption, Covington, Ky.*

100

bottom
God presents the Ten
Commandments to Moses.
The all-seeing Eye of God
crowns the composition.
*Window by Franz Mayer of
Munich, Germany, in Mother
of God Church, Covington, Ky.*

opposite page
God gives the Ten
Commandments to Moses
on Mount Sinai. *Detail of
window by F.X. Zettler of Munich,
Germany, in old St. Paul's Church,
Over-the-Rhine (now Verdin
Museum / Bell Event Center).*

THE TEN COMMANDMENTS

I am the LORD your God:
you shall not have strange Gods before me.

You shall not take the name
of the LORD your God in vain.

Remember to keep holy the LORD's Day.

Honor your father and your mother.

You shall not kill.

You shall not commit adultery.

You shall not steal.

You shall not bear false witness
against your neighbor.

You shall not covet your neighbor's wife.

You shall not covet your neighbor's goods.

THE GESTURE

Hand raised with two fingers bent. In Catholic art, a grouping of the fingers
in a 2 - 3 arrangement represents the fundamental truth that Jesus has two
natures (human and divine) and that there are three persons in one God.

opposite page
Italian marble statue in the foyer of the middle school
at The Summit Country Day School, Hyde Park.

above
His hand raised, Christ holds a young
child. *Window by F.X. Zettler of Munich,*
Germany, old LaSallette Academy Chapel
(now LaSallette Apartments, Covington, Ky).

top right
Detail of window by Tyrol Art Glass Company of
Innsbruck, Austria, in St. Joseph Church, West End.

bottom right
Detail of window by Riordan Art Glass,
Middletown, Oh, St. Andrew Church, Milford, Oh.

THE ETERNAL
CROSS

opposite page
Still life with processional
cross, illuminated by
light from a stained glass
window. *St. William Church,
West Price Hill.*

above
Series of crosses. From left:
Greek cross, Latin cross,
Egyptian or St. Anthony's
cross, Celtic cross, Cross
pommee, Roman cross.
*Window details by C.J.
Connick Associates of
Boston, Ma, in St. Mary
Church, Hyde Park.*

Chapter VI

STATIONS OF THE CROSS

JESUS IS TAKEN DOWN FROM THE CROSS

In this intricate and expressive artwork, Mary and the disciples tenderly wash Jesus' body
in preparation for burial. *Mosaic by Castaman of Venice, Italy, in Cathedral Basilica of the Assumption, Covington, Ky.*

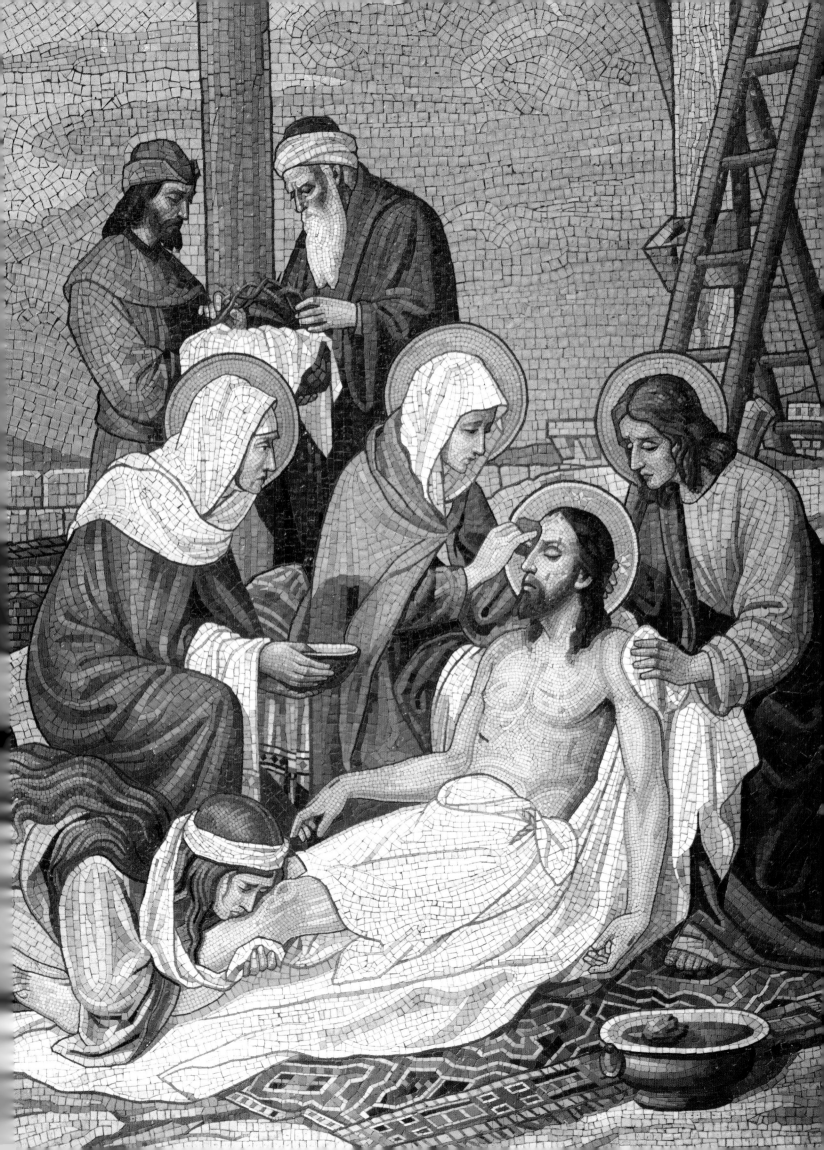

The walking of the Via Crucis (the Way of the Cross) in the Holy Land provided pilgrims the opportunity to make flesh in their lives what Saint Paul described as our "always carrying about in the body the dying of Jesus, so that the life of Jesus may also be manifested in our body" (see 2 Corinthians 4:10). When it was no longer practical or possible for people to travel to the Holy Land, representations of the Way of the Cross were placed in or near churches, so that the faithful could, through prayer and bodily gestures, commemorate the Passion of Jesus. Through the centuries, many have seen this devotion as a way of obeying the command of Jesus to take up the cross and follow Him (see Matthew 10:38, Luke 9:23 and 14:27).

Although the Stations of the Cross can be prayed at any time of the year, special attention is given them during Lent, when they are often prayed publicly. The stations provide a wonderful opportunity for the faithful to recognize the suffering Jesus in the poor and the suffering people of our day, wherever they are, and to touch them, as Jesus did, with hands that bring healing and peace.

JESUS IS CONDEMNED TO DEATH

Jesus stands solemnly to hear His death sentence, flanked by Pontius Pilate and a Roman centurion.
Painting by Anton Figel of Munich, Germany, St. Monica-St. George Church, Fairview Heights.

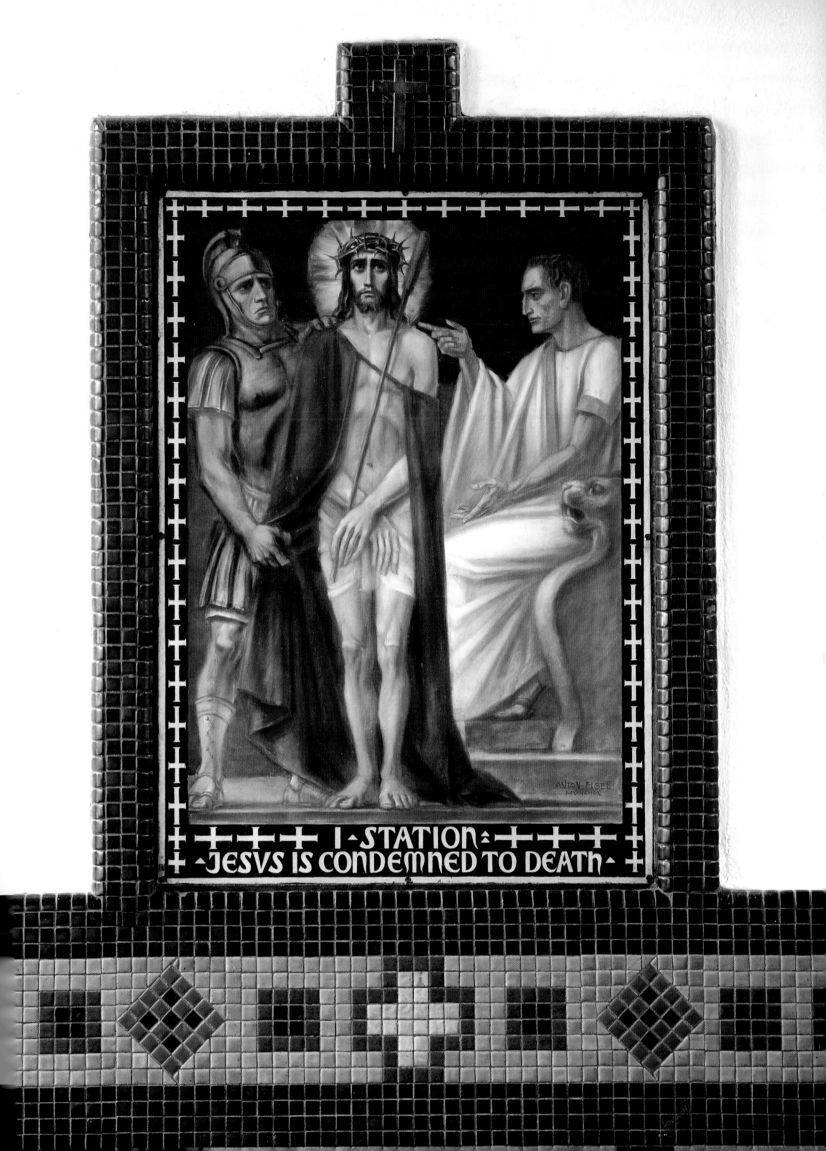

I · STATION
JESUS IS CONDEMNED TO DEATH

JESUS IS GIVEN HIS CROSS

opposite page

Jesus opens arms wide to accept His fate, as carpenters
raise the cross. *This Venetian glass mosaic is based on the 1898
paintings by Martin Von Feuerstein in St. Anna Church,
Munich, Germany, St. Boniface Church, Northside.*

JESUS FALLS THE FIRST TIME

above

Jesus stumbles under the weight of the cross.
*Cast plaster sculpture by Franz Mayer of Munich, Germany,
in St. Francis de Sales Church, East Walnut Hills.*

JESUS MEETS HIS MOTHER

A sorrowful Mary encounters her Son on the way
to Calvary. The vivid octagonal window features
a beaded frame. *Window by Riordan Art Glass,
Middletown, Oh, in the Church of the Annunciation, Clifton.*

SIMON OF CYRENE CARRIES THE CROSS

Simon of Cyrene, a town in Libya, is compelled by the Romans
to carry the cross for Jesus. For his role in the Passion, Simon
is celebrated as the first African saintly Christian.

Cast plaster sculpture in St. Lawrence Church, Price Hill.

114

VERONICA WIPES THE FACE OF JESUS

Veronica, whose name means "true likeness," wipes the face of Jesus,
leaving an image of His sorrowful visage on the cloth. She teaches us that
we see the true likeness of Christ when we help those who suffer. *Mosaic
by Castaman of Venice, Italy, in Cathedral Basilica of the Assumption, Covington, Ky.*

JESUS FALLS THE SECOND TIME

Against a lowering sky, Jesus falls once again, as a Roman soldier pulls
Him to His feet. *Oil on canvas, artist unknown, in St. Mark Church, Evanston.*

DAUGHTERS OF JERUSALEM

LUKE 23:27–31

A large crowd of people followed Jesus, including many women who mourned and lamented Him. Jesus turned to them and said, "Daughters of Jerusalem, do not weep for me; weep instead for yourselves and for your children, for indeed, the days are coming when people will say, 'Blessed are the barren, the wombs that never bore and the breasts that never nursed.' At that time, people will say to the mountains, 'Fall upon us!' and to the hills, 'Cover us!' for if these things are done when the wood is green what will happen when it is dry?"

117

JESUS MEETS THE WOMEN OF JERUSALEM

Sorrowing women fall to their knees and reach for Jesus. Even as He suffers He thinks of others. *Oil on canvas, artist unknown, in Mount St. Mary Seminary Chapel, Norwood, Oh (now Our Lady of the Holy Spirit Center).*

JESUS FALLS THE THIRD TIME

opposite page
Jesus collapses a final
time under the crushing
weight of the cross. *Cast plaster
sculpture in St. Francis Xavier
Church, downtown Cincinnati.*

JESUS IS STRIPPED OF HIS GARMENTS

right
Roman soldiers pull off
Jesus' clothes so they can
draw lots for them. *These
stations, by artist Carl Zimmerman,
were executed as part of the
renovation and expansion of the
Cathedral of St. Peter in Chains
in the 1950s, downtown Cincinnati.*

CRUCIFIXION: JESUS IS NAILED TO THE CROSS

Nails are pounded into Jesus' feet and hands as Mary looks on,
grief-stricken. *Hammered brass from P.H. Brunet & Cie, Paris, France,
in Sacred Heart Chapel, St. Anne's Convent, Melbourne, Ky.*

JESUS DIES ON THE CROSS

As Jesus dies on the cross, He gazes up toward His Father in heaven. The darkening
sky symbolizes pain and death, which will give way to the glorious Resurrection.

Mosaic by Vatican Studios, in St. Gregory the Great Chapel, Mount Washington.

JESUS' BODY IS REMOVED FROM THE CROSS

opposite page
Jesus lies in the care of His loving mother, whose
flowing red robe evokes His passion. *Mosaic by Vatican
Studios, in St. Gregory the Great Chapel, Mount Washington.*

right
Jesus is taken down from the cross. *Hammered
brass from P.H. Brunet & Cie, Paris, France, in Sacred
Heart Chapel, St. Anne's Convent, Melbourne, Ky.*

below
A heartbroken Mary gazes at the viewer. *This Venetian glass
mosaic is based on the 1898 paintings by Martin Von Feuerstein in
St. Anna Church, Munich, Germany, St. Boniface Church, Northside.*

124

JESUS IS LAID IN THE TOMB
AND COVERED IN INCENSE

above

Jesus' body is wrapped in burial cloths as Mary gently caresses His head. *Installed
in 1917, the mosaic by Castaman of Venice, Italy, reproduces an original oil painting by Bavarian
Redemptorist Brother Max Schmalzl. Cathedral Basilica of the Assumption, Covington, Ky.*

opposite page

Jesus' body is taken to the tomb by His disciples and accompanied by
Mary and Mary Magdalene. *Cast plaster relief by Joseph Sibbel, in Immaculate
Conception Chapel, Motherhouse of the Sisters of Charity, Delhi Township, Oh.*

Chapter VII

THE LIFE OF MARY

Wrapped in a pure white robe, Mary gazes down at the Infant Jesus.
Mosaic by Vatican Studios, in St. Gregory the Great Chapel, Mount Washington.

I n the time when Mary was born, the name 'Galilee' was associated with broken hearts and broken promises, and many wondered what good could come from there. It was to Galilee, the place of great hurt and disappointment, that God's strength went to announce the Good News.

Gabriel announced that new life would come to Mary, a young woman betrothed but not yet married. The new life will be Jesus ("YHWH saves"). When Mary naturally inquired how this could be, God's strength answered that The Holy Spirit will come upon thee, and that her son will be the Son of God. To all this, Mary answered yes.

The story does not end here. Once God's word entered Mary, she could not remain where she was. She went to the hill country and entered the house of Zechariah and found Elizabeth. When Elizabeth heard Mary's voice, she felt new life stir within her, and when Elizabeth declared Mary blessed, Mary answered with her Magnificat, declaring that all praise belongs to God.

Mary remained completely faithful to the word that she shared with the world. Her life of devotion is an inspiration to all of us to remain faithful to the word, to share it with the world, and to follow it faithfully wherever it leads us.

Mary gazes in awe to God as cherubim bear palms and lilies. *Window by Emil Frei Stained Glass of St. Louis, Mo, in St. Ursula Academy Chapel, East Walnut Hills.*

opposite page
St. Anne, mother of
Mary, holds her daughter
as she inscribes a holy text.
Neo-Gothic window by C.J.
Connick Associates of Boston, Ma,
in St. Mary Church, Hyde Park.

left
The child Mary is
presented in the temple.
In the apocryphal literature,
Anna and Joachim offered
Mary to God when she was
three years old, to fulfill a
promise made to God when
Anna was still childless.
Window by Tyrol Art Glass
Company of Innsbruck, Austria,
in St. Joseph Church, West End.

As Mary kneels in prayer, an angel announces that she has been chosen to be the mother of Jesus. *Window by Franz Mayer of Munich, Germany. Formerly in the Church of the Assumption, Walnut Hills, it is now in storage.*

132

Lavish ten-pointed rose window. *By Franz Mayer of Munich, Germany, St. Andrew Church, Avondale.*

HAIL MARY

Hail Mary, full of grace;
the Lord is with thee:
blessed art thou among women, and
blessed is the fruit of thy womb, Jesus.
Holy Mary, Mother of God,
pray for us sinners,
now and at the hour of our death.

Amen.

above
Relief attributed to Rookwood Pottery,
St. Agnes Church, Fort Wright, Ky.

opposite page
"Motherhood." A mother tenderly kisses the
infant on her lap. The statue can also be seen
as a tribute to the Madonna. *Italian white marble*
sculpture in St. Anne Convent Cemetery, Melbourne, Ky.

❦ APPARITIONS OF MARY ❦

OUR LADY OF FATIMA

opposite page

In 1917, three Portuguese children experienced visions
of Mary, who asked them to pray the rosary for peace,
the end of World War I and the conversion of Russia.
*Neo-Gothic windows by C.J. Connick Associates of Boston, Ma,
in the former Ursuline Academy Chapel, Walnut Hills.*

OUR LADY OF LOURDES

top

In 1858, Mary appeared to Bernadette Soubirous, a poor
and sickly French peasant girl. Lourdes became a worldwide
place of faith, pilgrimage and healing. *Window by Riordan Art
Glass, Middletown, Oh, in the Church of the Annunciation, Clifton.*

OUR LADY OF GUADALUPE

bottom

In December 1531, Mary appeared to Mexican peasant
Juan Diego. Dressed as an Aztec princess, she asked that a
church be built on the spot. Our Lady of Guadalupe is the
patron saint of Mexico and the Americas. *Window by Riordan
Art Glass, Middletown, Oh, in the Church of the Annunciation, Clifton.*

top
Mary and the Infant Jesus. *Detail of window by F.X. Zettler of Munich, Germany, in St. Francis de Sales Church, East Walnut Hills.*

bottom
This window depicts the wedding of Mary and Joseph: an event rarely depicted in art. *Window by Franz Mayer of Munich, Germany, in Cathedral Basilica of the Assumption, Covington, Ky.*

opposite page
Haloed by a star, Mary gazes directly at the viewer, hands clasped in prayer. *Art Deco stone relief, St. William Church, West Price Hill.*

THE MEMORARE

Remember, O most loving Virgin Mary,
that never was it known that anyone who fled to your protection,
implored your help, or sought your intercession
was left unaided.

Inspired with this confidence,
we turn to you, O Virgin of virgins, our Mother.
To you we come, before you we stand, sinful and sorrowful.

O Mother of the Word Incarnate,
do not despise our petitions,
but in your mercy hear us and answer us.

Amen.

above

"A great sign appeared in the sky, a woman clothed with the
sun, with the moon under her feet, and on her head a crown
of twelve stars" (Revelation 12:1). After her assumption,
Mary is hailed as Regina Coeli, Queen of Heaven.
Mural, artist unknown, St. Clare Convent Chapel, Hartwell.

opposite page

Mary kneels humbly before her Son, who bears her crown
and scepter. *Window by Tyrol Art Glass Company of Innsbruck,
Austria, in St. Joseph Church, West End.*

Chapter VIII

MYSTERIES OF THE ROSARY

THE ASSUMPTION OF MARY

Angels, Saints and God the Father, who is rarely depicted in art, welcome
Mary into heaven. *Mural painted by W. Lamprecht in 1901; repainted by Wilhelm, 1950.*
Immaculate Conception Chapel, Motherhouse of the Sisters of Charity, Delhi Township, Oh.

IN UMBRA MANUS SUAE PROTEXIT ME

n many monasteries, the custom of praying the 150 psalms of the Book of Psalms was adapted for the members of the community who could not read. Instead of chanting the psalms, these members were encouraged to pray one *Ave* (as the Hail Mary was known) for each psalm. To help keep track of these prayers, they were divided into three groups of 50, the latter being further divided into five groups of 10. Those who recited these prayers often held in their hands a garland (in Latin, rosarium) to remind them of the number of prayers said.

The three groups of 50 *Aves* became associated with certain mysteries in the life of Jesus: the Joyful, the Sorrowful, and the Glorious. In October 2002, Blessed John Paul II introduced a fourth set of mysteries, knows as the Luminous Mysteries. These are: The Baptism of Jesus, the Wedding at Cana, the Proclamation of the Kingdom, the Transfiguration, and the Institution of the Eucharist.

The Rosary has sustained many people in their faith. Its simple structure and ease of use allow us to be drawn deeply into the mystery of salvation.

THE SCOURGING AT THE PILLAR

As a prelude to His crucifixion, Jesus is beaten with flails.
Window by F.X. Zettler of Munich, Germany, in Mount St. Mary Seminary Chapel, Norwood, Oh (now Our Lady of the Holy Spirit Center).

JOYFUL MYSTERIES

THE ANNUNCIATION

right

The Holy Spirit descends on Mary as an angel tells momentous news: she will be the mother of Jesus. *Window by Emil Frei Stained Glass of St. Louis, Mo, in St. Ursula Academy Chapel, East Walnut Hills.*

THE VISITATION

opposite page

Immediately after the Annunciation, Mary travels to visit her cousin, Elizabeth, who is pregnant with John the Baptist. *Window by Franz Mayer of Munich, Germany, in Immaculate Conception Chapel, Motherhouse of the Sisters of Charity, Delhi Township, Oh.*

THE GIFT OF MR AND MRS BELLAMY STORER

GLORIA

Glory to God in the highest. And on earth peace to men of good will.
We praise You. We bless You. We adore You. We glorify You.
We give You thanks for Your great glory.
O Lord God, heavenly King, God the Father almighty.
O Lord Jesus Christ, the Only-begotten Son.
O Lord God, Lamb of God, Son of the Father:
You Who take away the sins of the world, have mercy on us.
You Who take away the sins of the world, receive our prayer.
You Who sit at the right hand of the Father, have mercy on us.
For You alone are holy. You alone are the Lord.
You alone, O Jesus Christ, are most high.
Together with the Holy Spirit in the glory of God the Father.

Amen.

THE NATIVITY

right

On a starry Christmas night, the Holy Family and an angel worship Baby Jesus in a thatched-roof stable. *Window by Franz Mayer of Munich, Germany, in Immaculate Conception Chapel, Motherhouse of the Sisters of Charity, Delhi Township, Oh.*

THE PRESENTATION

opposite page

In accordance with Jewish law, Mary and Joseph present the Infant Jesus in the temple forty days after His birth. *Window by Emil Frei Stained Glass of St. Louis, Mo, in St. Ursula Academy Chapel, East Walnut Hills.*

THE FINDING OF THE
CHILD JESUS IN THE TEMPLE

above
Jesus teaching in the temple. *Window by Tyrol Art Glass
Company of Innsbruck, Austria, in St. Joseph Church, West End.*

opposite page
After Mary and Joseph left the temple at Passover, the 12-year-old Jesus lingered among
the elders, who were amazed at His learning. *Window by Franz Mayer of Munich, Germany,
in Immaculate Conception Chapel, Motherhouse of the Sisters of Charity, Delhi Township, Oh.*

151

THE BAPTISM

opposite page

Jesus is baptized in the
Jordan River by John the
Baptist. *Window originally
in Corpus Christi Church,
Newport, Ky, relocated to All
Saints Church, Walton, Ky.*

THE WEDDING

left

The wedding feast at
Cana was Jesus' first public
miracle. This window, by
F.X. Zettler of Munich,
Germany, won first place
at the World's Columbian
Exposition in Chicago, Il,
in 1893. *Old St. Paul's Church,
Over-the-Rhine (now Verdin
Museum / Bell Event Center).*

153

top left
Quatrefoil with golden
chalice and host. *Sisters
of Notre Dame de Namur
Chapel, Reading, Oh.*

top right
Oval relief with chalice,
radiant host and embossed
border. *St. William Church,
West Price Hill.*

bottom left
In a hexagonal medallion
filled with grape leaves, an
ornate chalice rests on the
Bible. *Detail of window created in
Munich, Germany, in Immaculate
Heart of Mary Chapel, The Summit
Country Day School, Hyde Park.*

bottom right
Chalice against a field
of glowing gold. *Window
by Franz Mayer of Munich,
Germany, in old St. George
Church, Clifton Heights.*

154

THE HOLY EUCHARIST

LUKE 22:17–20

Then He took a cup, gave thanks, and said,
"Take this and share it among yourselves;

for I tell you (that) from this time on I shall not drink
of the fruit of the vine until the kingdom of God comes."

Then He took the bread, said the blessing, broke it,
and gave it to them, saying, "This is my body,
which will be given for you; do this in memory of me."

And likewise the cup after they had eaten,
saying, "This cup is the new covenant
in my blood, which will be shed for you."

THE LAST SUPPER

Recorded in all four Gospels, the Last Supper was Jesus' final meal with the
apostles before the crucifixion. *Detail of window by Franz Mayer of Munich, Germany,
in Immaculate Conception Chapel, Motherhouse of the Sisters of Charity, Delhi Township, Oh.*

THE PROCLAMATION OF THE KINGDOM

opposite page

(Acts 28:31). St. Luke's Acts of the Apostles tells how St. Paul
boldly preached the kingdom of God. *Window by Franz Mayer
of Munich, Germany, in old St. George Church, Clifton Heights*

THE TRANSFIGURATION

above

Jesus, accompanied by Moses and Elijah, radiates the glory of God.
Mural by Leon Lippert in Sacred Heart Church, Bellevue, Ky (now Divine Mercy Parish).

SORROWFUL MYSTERIES

THE AGONY
OF JESUS IN
THE GARDEN

opposite page
Ten-sided Renaissance-
style rose window of richly
enameled glass, relieved by a
border of trefoils. *Window by
Franz Mayer of Munich, Germany,
in St. Andrew Church, Avondale.*

THE SCOURGING
AT THE PILLAR

right
Bound to a pillar painted purple
(the color of martyrdom),
Jesus gazes at the viewer.
*Detail of window by Franz Mayer
of Munich, Germany, in St. Andrew
Church, Avondale.*

THE CROWNING
OF THORNS

opposite page
"And Pilate said to them,
Behold the man!" (John 19:2).
Jesus, robed in red, is
crowned with woven thorn
branches in mockery of His
kingship, a stalk placed in
His hand in lieu of a scepter.
*Window by F.X. Zettler of
Munich, Germany, in Mount
St. Mary Seminary Chapel,
Norwood, Oh (now Our Lady
of the Holy Spirit Center).*

right
Robed in purple by the
Romans, hands bound, the
thorn-crowned Jesus gazes
out at the viewer. *Window by
Franz Mayer of Munich, Germany,
in St. Andrew Church, Avondale.*

THE CARRYING OF THE CROSS

opposite page

Jesus stumbles under the crushing weight of the cross.
Window by F.X. Zettler of Munich, Germany, in Mount St. Mary Seminary
Chapel, Norwood, Oh (now Our Lady of the Holy Spirit Center).

THE CRUCIFIXION

above

Jesus dies on the cross, flanked by Mary and St. John the beloved
disciple. Byzantine-style icon. *Created by Jenny Ward, Cincinnati, Oh.*

GLORIOUS
MYSTERIES

THE
RESURRECTION

right
On the third day, Jesus
rises in glory from the dead,
astonishing the soldiers
guarding the tomb. *Window
by F.X. Zettler of Munich,
Germany, in old St. Paul's Church,
Over-the-Rhine (now Verdin
Museum / Bell Event Center).*

THE ASCENSION

opposite page
The risen Jesus ascends
to heaven, attended by
worshipful saints and angels.
*Window by Emil Frei Stained
Glass of St. Louis, Mo, in St.
Lawrence Church, Price Hill.*

164

THE DESCENT OF THE HOLY SPIRIT

above

Pentecost commemorates the descent of the Holy Spirit upon Mary and the disciples
after the Resurrection of Jesus. *Window by Franz Mayer of Munich, Germany, in Immaculate
Conception Chapel, Motherhouse of the Sisters of Charity, Delhi Township, Oh.*

THE ASSUMPTION OF MARY

opposite page

A worshipful Mary rises into a golden cloud filled with cherubim. *Window by Riordan Art
Glass of Middletown, Oh, in St. Matthew Church, Norwood, Oh (now Immaculate Conception Parish).*

THE CORONATION OF MARY

above

Jesus crowns the humbly bowed head of His mother,
seated beside Him on the golden celestial throne. *Window
by Radiant Arts, Beach City, Oh, in All Saints Church, Walton, Ky.*

opposite page

God the Father, the Son and the Holy Spirit, place the crown of heaven on
the bowed head of Mary. *Window by Franz Mayer of Munich, Germany, in Immaculate
Conception Chapel, Motherhouse of the Sisters of Charity, Delhi Township, Oh.*

HAIL HOLY QUEEN

Hail, holy Queen, Mother of mercy,
hail, our life, our sweetness and our hope.
To thee do we cry, poor banished children of Eve:
to thee do we send up our sighs,
mourning and weeping in this vale of tears.
Turn then, most gracious Advocate,
thine eyes of mercy toward us,
and after this our exile,
show unto us the blessed fruit of thy womb, Jesus,
O merciful, O loving, O sweet Virgin Mary!

Amen.

Chapter IX

THE HOLY FAMILY

This complex and visually arresting window traces the lineage of Mary
and Joseph through the lines of Isaac, Judas, Jacob and David. *Window
by Franz Mayer of Munich, Germany, in Mother of God Church, Covington, Ky.*

lthough devotion to the Holy Family (under that title) does not appear until the seventeenth century, and the Feast was not placed in the Latin Rite Calendar until 1921 under Pope Benedict XV, the list of those who depicted the Holy Family in art contains many famous names. Michelangelo, da Vinci, Raphael, Rembrandt, Rubens, Titian, and Van Dyck are but some of those who could be mentioned.

Catholic tradition places great emphasis on the family's role in Church and society. The prayers at Mass for the Feast of the Holy Family remind us that Jesus, Mary, and Joseph are models for our living, playing, and working with others.

We do not know the details of the daily life of the Holy Family. We do know that Joseph and Mary loved and cherished the gift from God that was Jesus, and we know that Jesus grew up in Nazareth, obedient to Mary and Joseph, and filled with wisdom (see Luke 2:40, 51–52). We do know that the members of the Holy Family loved each other and that they remained faithful to their calling. If future generations do not know our daily routines, our likes and dislikes, but know that we loved each other and were faithful to God's will, perhaps they will know about us what is most important to know about any human being.

The Adoration of the Shepherds. In this brilliantly shaded panel, reverent shepherds kneel by the newborn Jesus. *Window by F.X. Zettler of Munich, Germany, in old St. Paul's Church, Over-the-Rhine (now Verdin Museum / Bell Event Center).*

SILENT NIGHT

Silent night, holy night, All is calm, all is bright
Round yon Virgin Mother and Child, Holy Infant so tender and mild
Sleep in heavenly peace, Sleep in heavenly peace

Silent night, holy night! Shepherds quake at the sight
Glories stream from heaven afar, Heavenly hosts sing Alleluia!
Christ, the Saviour is born, Christ, the Saviour is born

Silent night, holy night, Son of God, love's pure light
Radiant beams from Thy holy face, With the dawn of redeeming grace
Jesus, Lord, at Thy birth, Jesus, Lord, at Thy birth

above
The Christmas star beams over the sleeping
town, wreathed in olive blossoms. *Window
maker unknown, in St. Gabriel Church, Glendale, Oh.*

opposite page
Suffused with rich tones, this window depicts the
wedding of Mary and Joseph. *Window by Franz Mayer
of Munich, Germany in Mother of God Church, Covington, Ky.*

opposite page
A lushly painted Nativity
scene depicts Mary and
garlanded adoring angels
kneeling by the sleeping
Child Jesus. *Window by
Franz Mayer of Munich,
Germany, in old St. George
Church, Clifton Heights.*

left
Two brocaded angels
serenade the Christ Child on
lute and violin. *Window by Emil
Frei Stained Glass of St. Louis, Mo,
in St. Lawrence Church, Price Hill.*

177

opposite page
Under cover of night, the Holy Family flees Bethlehem.
*Window by F.X. Zettler of Munich, Germany in old St. Paul's Church,
Over-the-Rhine (now Verdin Museum / Bell Event Center).*

above
In this imagined scene, the Holy Family meets with Mary's
cousin, Elizabeth, her husband, Zachariah, and their son,
John the Baptist. *Window by Franz Mayer of Munich, Germany,
in Mother of God Church, Covington, Ky.*

left
The Child Jesus preaches
the Fourth Commandment,
Honor Thy Father and Thy
Mother, to children gathered
in a lush garden. *Window in
St. Aloysius Church (maker
unknown), Elmwood Place, Oh
(now Our Lady of Lavang Parish).*

opposite page
St. Joseph and the Christ
Child, solemnly side by
side. *Mosaic, maker unknown,
in St. Gregory the Great Chapel,
Mount Washington.*

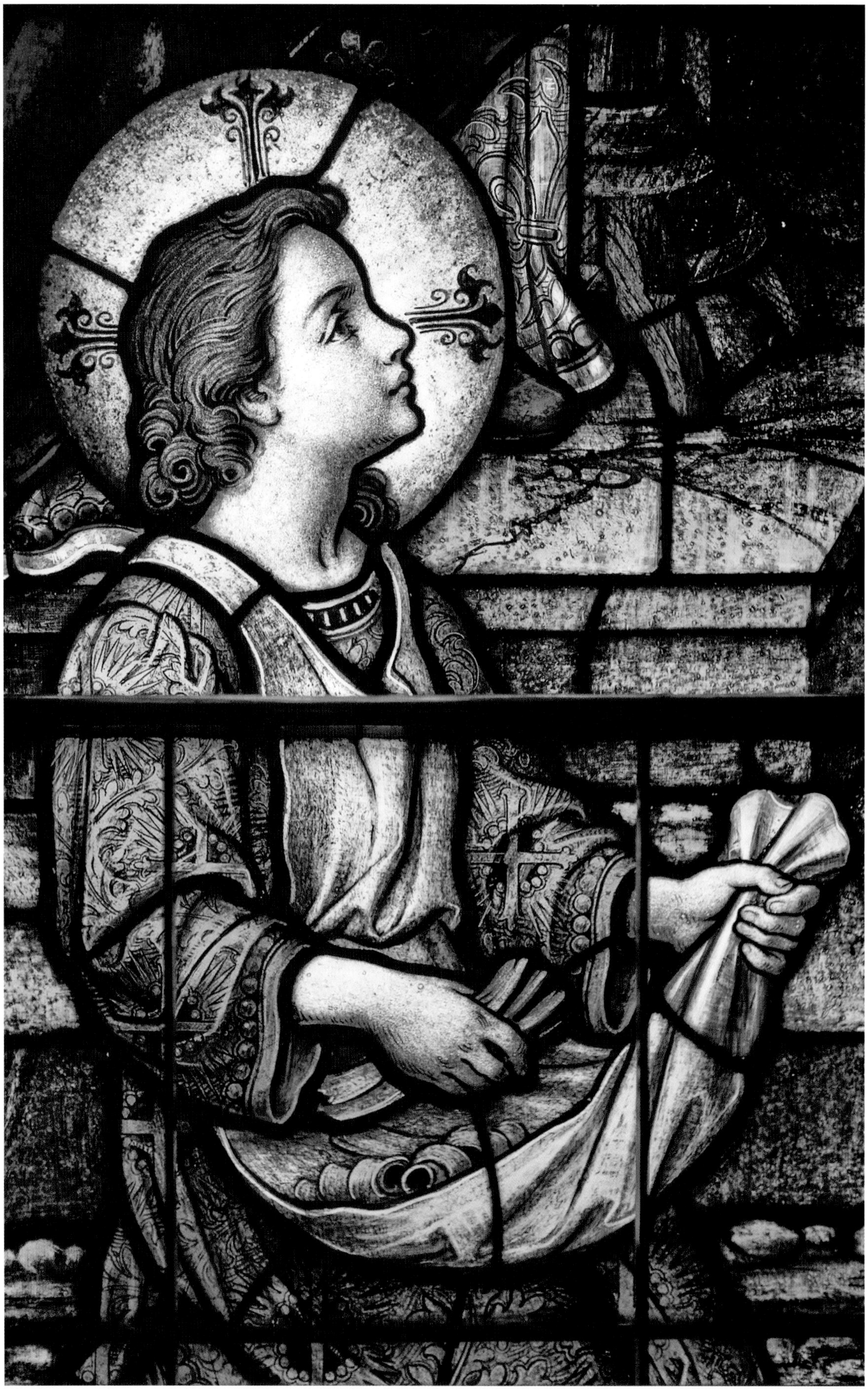

183

The everyday life of the
Holy Family is the subject of
this impressionistic mural.
*Mural by Leon Lippert in Sacred
Heart Church, Bellevue, Ky
(now Divine Mercy Parish).*

185

Chapter X

THE LIFE OF CHRIST

"Let the little children come to me, and do not prevent them; for the
kingdom of heaven belongs to such as these" (Matthew 19:14). Mothers
present their children to Jesus as two disapproving disciples look on.
Window by Emil Frei Stained Glass of St. Louis, Mo, in St. Lawrence Church, Price Hill.

188

n keeping communion with His people, God, who Himself is a communion of persons, gave the world His only begotten Son. In God's own Son, Jesus, God found one who would listen, one whose answer to God was always "yes" (see 2 Corinthians 1:19).

Jesus' "yes" to His Father's will is the model for all of us. He is the model for children, called to be obedient to their parents. He is the model for young people, who must discern their gifts and their calling. He is the model for adults, who, in fidelity to their specific vocation, must serve others humbly. He is the model for the elderly, who, after a life of faithful service, must embrace bodily death to enter eternal life.

In the Resurrection of Jesus, humanity is raised to new life. In His Ascension to heaven, humanity is now seated at God's right hand. When He returns in glory, it will be to gather the faithful into His Heavenly Kingdom. What we lost in the garden of Eden, was restored to us in the garden where Jesus was laid in the tomb. Mary Magdalene went to that garden, early in the morning on the first day of the week (see John 20:1). Expecting to find death, she instead found the risen Christ, who sent her forth to bring the good news to those who would eventually spread this "Word of God" throughout the entire world.

"I am the good shepherd; the good shepherd lays down His life for the sheep" (John 10:11). *Window by Emil Frei Stained Glass of St. Louis, Mo, in St. Ursula Academy Chapel, East Walnut Hills.*

above
The Child Jesus holds a wooden cross as Mary and Joseph look on in
wonder. *Window designed by William Zettler of Riordan Art Glass of Middletown,*
Oh, in St. Matthew Church, Norwood, Oh (now Immaculate Conception Parish).

opposite page
"And He said to them, 'Why were you looking for me? Did you not know
that I must be in my Father's house?'" (Luke 2:49). *Window by F.X. Zettler*
of Munich, Germany, in St. Francis de Sales Church, East Walnut Hills.

OUR FATHER

Our Father, Who art in heaven,
hallowed be Thy name;
Thy kingdom come;
Thy will be done,
on earth as it is in heaven.
Give us this day our daily bread;
and forgive us our trespasses
as we forgive those who trespass against us;
and lead us not into temptation,
but deliver us from evil. Amen.

opposite page
Jesus is afloat with the apostles on a roiling sea, whose
deep water symbolizes chaos. *Window by Franz Mayer
of Munich, Germany, in St. Andrew Church, Avondale.*

above
"Come after me, and I will make you fishers of men"
(Mark 1:17 and Matthew 4:19). *Mural by Leon Lippert in
Sacred Heart Church, Bellevue, Ky (now Divine Mercy Parish).*

MATTHEW 19:13–15

Then children were brought to Him that He might lay
His hands on them and pray. The disciples rebuked them,

but Jesus said, "Let the children come to me, and do not prevent
them; for the kingdom of heaven belongs to such as these."

After He placed His hands on them, He went away.

194

above
Children and their mothers surround Jesus. *Detail of window
by Riordan Art Glass of Middletown, Oh, in Immaculate Conception
Chapel, Motherhouse of the Sisters of Charity, Delhi Township, Oh.*

opposite page
Arms open wide, Jesus welcomes infants and children, as
their mothers kneel before Him. *Window by Emil Frei Stained
Glass of St. Louis, Mo, in St. Ursula Academy Chapel, East Walnut Hills.*

◈ JESUS ENTERS JERUSALEM ◈

MARK 11:9–10

Those preceding Him as well as those following kept crying out:
"Hosanna! Blessed is He who comes in the name of the Lord!

Blessed is the kingdom of our father David that is to come! Hosanna in the highest!"

Jesus rides into Jerusalem in triumph as cheering crowds lay down cloaks, palm and tree branches before Him. Traditionally, Jesus' arrival on a donkey instead of a horse suggests He came in peace. *Mural by Leon Lippert in Sacred Heart Church, Bellevue, Ky (now Divine Mercy Parish).*

GIFT OF THE SISTERS, GLOCKNER SANITARIUM, COLORADO SPRINGS

opposite page
Jesus lays His healing hands
on the sick clustered about
His feet, touching His cloak.
*Window by Franz Mayer
of Munich, Germany, in
Immaculate Conception Chapel,
Motherhouse of the Sisters of
Charity, Delhi Township, Oh.*

left
Jesus blesses St. Joseph on
his deathbed as Mary looks
on. St. Joseph is the patron of
a happy death. *Window by Emil
Frei Stained Glass of St. Louis, Mo,
in Holy Family Church, Price Hill.*

opposite page
The house of Mary
and Martha. Mary the
contemplative sits at Jesus'
feet to hear the word of God,
as practical Martha brings a
tray of food she has prepared.
*Window by Franz Mayer of
Munich, Germany, in St. Andrew
Church, Avondale.*

right
Jesus appears after His
Resurrection, giving His
disciples the gift of the Holy
Spirit (John 20:22–23).
*Window by Franz Mayer of
Munich, Germany, in old St.
George Church, Clifton Heights.*

Receive ye the Holy Ghost. Whose sins
you shall forgive them, and whose sins
they are retained John XX, 22, 23.

NICENE CREED

We believe in one God,
the Father, the Almighty,
maker of heaven and earth,
of all that is seen and unseen.

We believe in one Lord, Jesus Christ,
the only Son of God,
eternally begotten of the Father,
God from God, Light from Light,
true God from true God,
begotten, not made,
one in Being with the Father.
Through Him all things were made.
For us men and for our salvation
He came down from heaven:
by the power of the Holy Spirit
He was born of the Virgin Mary,
and became man.

For our sake He was crucified under Pontius Pilate,
He suffered, died, and was buried.
On the third day He rose again
in fulfillment of the Scriptures;
He ascended into heaven
and is seated at the right hand of the Father.
He will come again in glory
to judge the living and the dead,
and His kingdom will have no end.

We believe in the Holy Spirit, the Lord, the giver of life,
who proceeds from the Father and the Son.
With the Father and the Son
He is worshiped and glorified.
He has spoken through the Prophets.
We believe in one holy catholic and apostolic Church.
We acknowledge one baptism for the forgiveness of sins.
We look for the resurrection of the dead
and the life of the world to come. Amen.

203

The risen Jesus bursts forth in glory from the tomb, witnessed
by an angel, as the waiting Romans recoil in fear and amazement
(Matthew 28:2–10). *Window by Franz Mayer of Munich, Germany,
in the Cathedral Basilica of the Assumption, Covington, Ky.*

AFTERWORD

BY ROBERT A. FLISCHEL

The origins of this project date back more than twenty years. During the late 1970s and early 1980s I was photographing a fair number of weddings and religious services throughout Cincinnati and Northern Kentucky. I found myself working in small chapels, historic temples, beautiful churches and even an occasional basilica or cathedral. The question arose... how many people have seen or were even aware of these remarkable spaces? The more churches I visited, the greater the desire became to examine them in more detail. Thus the journey began, one of discovery, exploration and understanding, with a goal of telling a clear and meaningful story.

Even though the style and grandeur of these structures was magnificent, I decided to not make architecture the focus. While I searched for a stronger storyline, this project made its way to the back burner as I developed and published other books. Gradually over time, I returned again and again to the "church project." After hundreds of photographs and dozens of scouting trips, the story emerged. I decided to create a book using the art in over 50 Catholic churches and chapels in Cincinnati and Northern Kentucky that tell the story of the Roman Catholic faith. After all, this area represented the perfect microcosm of a major movement in America between 1840 and 1950. Thousands of German and Irish immigrants, as well as Greeks, Italians and French were filling the major cities all across America. They brought their faith, their skills, and above all, their energy and desire to help build their communities.

Now the pieces were in place, it was time to photograph this collection of world art. The process was exhilarating and occasionally exasperating. The final key for me was building a photographic team to work with. I didn't have to look far; they were right at hand. Trusted associates

Joe Simon, Jay Yocis and color specialist Lorena Gomez Mostajo contributed immensely to this process. As we worked another issue became crystal clear; much of this art is presently endangered. Even as I saw remarkable efforts by the Archdiocese of Cincinnati and the Diocese of Covington to preserve and restore this irreplaceable art, the combination of parish closings, wear and tear from the elements, and the magnitude of the collection itself make this a daunting challenge. My hope is that this book can raise awareness and become as inspiring for the viewer as it was for my whole team.

Throughout the process we were guided by the words of Emile Male, from his classic work written in 1898, *The Gothic Image, Religious Art in France of the Thirteenth Century,* "But this is a transfigured world, where light is more dazzling than in ordinary life, and shadow more mysterious."

The early work on this project was done with Nikon film cameras, primarily F3's & F5's, all with Nikkor lenses. Film was primarily Fujichrome Velvia, RVP 135. As digital imaging improved Robert Flischel & Joe Simon used the Nikon D300 and D700. Jay Yocis preferred the Olympus E5. All digital images were shot in the "RAW" mode. Photographing stained glass windows is always a challenge for several reasons; the exteriors are affected by industrial grime & soot, while the interiors are affected by dust & smoke. Faithful replication of these windows is a balancing act. Suffice to say we use many techniques in the post production processes to create as faithful a reproduction as possible.

A series of medieval themed floor tiles. *Created by the Moravian Pottery & Tile Works, Doylestown, Pa, in St. Mary Church, Hyde Park.*

ACKNOWLEDGEMENTS

The degree of "teamwork" necessary to complete this book cannot be underestimated. All aspects of this project were dependant on this principle.

My love and gratitude to my wife Jackie and daughter Emma for their love, support and assistance throughout the project. Also my appreciation and love to my niece and managing editor, Mara Mulvihill, for all of the remarkable work she patiently and expertly performed.

This project was energized when The Carol Ann and Ralph V. Haile, Jr. U.S. Bank Foundation made a commitment to the book. Thanks to Chris Bochenek and the entire Haile team for their continued support. The next major boost occurred when I shared my story with Kim David, a board member at The Summit Country Day School. Kim, a rare individual with vision and a "roll your sleeves up" attitude, immediately pledged her support to all phases of the project. My Alma Mater, Xavier University provided the final production support when they agreed to be the presenting sponsor. My sincere thanks to President Michael J. Graham, S.J., and his entire team for their vision and enthusiasm.

With these commitments I immediately turned to Madison Design Group in Covington, Kentucky. What an enriching experience it was working with this talented organization. With Allison and Lindsey as principal designers and with support from Tricia, Sarah, Sean, Jonathan, Julie, Jackie and Charlotte, this story was brought to life.

It is important for me to acknowledge the impact of associate photographers Joe Simon and Jay Yocis. Their effort was monumental in making this story a reality.

Margo Warminski joined the team as a superlative researcher and writer and remained a key contributor throughout. I was empowered by the considerable talent and support offered by Bill and Anne Burleigh. Anne wrote the heartfelt preface and both served as editorial guides. Along the way Bill and Anne introduced me to Monsignor William Cleves, who wrote the inspirational essays that open each chapter. Reverend Chris Armstrong, advisor to the project since 1996, provided the moving introduction.

The post production team was ably led by Lorena Gomez Mostajo. She was assisted along the way by Monte Davis from Pixels and Dots Design, Linda Schardine from Robin Imaging and long-time associate Jennifer Schiller.

A special thank you to Thomas McKiernan, an early supporter, who guided me through the wild and wonderful "West Side" of Cincinnati. He also listened patiently and calmly to my "litany" of struggles pertaining to the book-making process.

My editorial support team consisted of Emily Jolly who expertly and enthusiastically guided me through some very choppy waters. Emily's niece, Suzi Jolly, served us well as a problem solver and marketing advisor. I was fortunate to have historian Robert Vitz, Ph.D., provide clear and coherent advice on a variety of important subjects. Many thanks to Gavin Meyer, who did everything from photo assisting to index editing. The all-around effort provided by intern Trevyn Riley was also a boost.

Without question, I am grateful to the "open door" policy made possible by the Archdiocese of Cincinnati and the Diocese of Covington, Ky. The leadership provided by Archbishop Dennis M. Schnurr and Bishop Roger J. Foys was vital to the process. I was, without exception, warmly welcomed by all the clergy, religious and laity from all the parishes we visited. A tip of the cap to Dan Andriatico and Archivists Don Buske and Thomas Kennealy, S.J., for their gracious assistance.

I also need to recognize Dean Sherman from Oceanic Printing for his guidance. Jay and Sheree Allgood provided excellent Biblical insights.

The Executive Committee was a great asset. Members Scott David, Tom McKiernan, Reverend Phil Seher, Conky Greiwe and Pat Gaito were indispensable throughout the entire project.

Jesus, Father of all nations, bronze relief, entrance façade at Our Lady of Visitation Church, Mack, Oh.

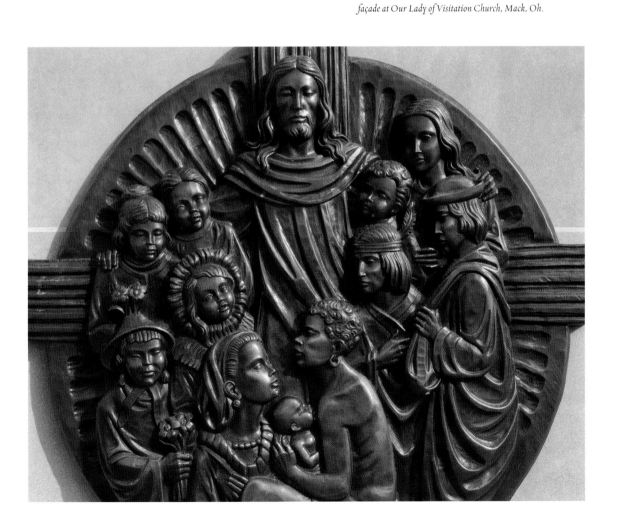

SPONSORS

PRESENTED BY

Xavier University

ROSE

The Carol Ann and Ralph V. Haile, Jr.,
U.S. Bank Foundation

Madison Design Group

DOVE

James J. and Joan A. Gardner

LILY

Anne and Bill Burleigh

Fran and Wayne Carlisle

Kim and Scott David

Tom Schiff

SHAMROCK

Jinny and John Berten

Mary Dean Grote

Thomas McKiernan

Nadine Whitsett

ANGEL

Mr. and Mrs. William Butler

Mr. and Mrs. Robert Kohlhepp

SUNFLOWER

Helen Adams and
Patrick Borders

Nancy Berlier

Joe and Mary Brinkmeyer

Bob and Dianne Donnelly

Betsy Flischel and
Tom and Jamie Gustina

Madeline and Patrick Gilligan

Tom and Toots Klippstein

Duke and Mary McGonegle

Bill and Linda O'Donnell
and Family

Dean and Marilyn Sherman

Ann and Joe Wilmers

Blessed Mother in carved wood, Cathedral
Basilica of the Assumption, Covington, Ky.

CONTRIBUTORS

REVEREND CHRISTOPHER ARMSTRONG

Rev. Christopher Armstrong has been a priest of the Archdiocese of Cincinnati for over 30 years. He is currently the pastor of St. Antoninus parish on the west side of Cincinnati.

ANNE HUSTED BURLEIGH

Anne Husted Burleigh is a freelance writer, wife of 47 years, mother, and grandmother, who lives in Rabbit Hash, Kentucky. She has written many articles and columns for such publications as *Modern Age*; *Intercollegiate Review*; *Crisis Magazine*; *Magnificat*; *Catholic Dossier*; *Canticle*; *Homiletic & Pastoral Review*; *National Catholic Register*; *Sacred Architecture*; and *Communio*. She is the author of *Journey up the River, A Midwesterner's Spiritual Pilgrimage* (Ignatius Press) and *John Adams* (Transaction Publishers). She is also the editor of *Education in a Free Society* (Liberty Fund). Anne has published numerous pieces on Wendell Berry and is a contributor to the forthcoming book, *The Humane Vision of Wendell Berry* (ISI Books).

MONSIGNOR WILLIAM CLEVES

Msgr. William Cleves is a priest of the diocese of Covington. He entered seminary studies after high school, studying at Saint Pius X Seminary, the Athenaeum of Ohio, and the Pontifical Gregorian University in Rome, Italy. He taught at Thomas More College in Crestview Hills, Kentucky for 24 years, and served as president for nine. For five years he served the Pontifical College Josephinum in Columbus, Ohio as Director of Spiritual Formation and Vice Rector of the School of Theology. He is the author of *Stories in Glass: The Windows of the Cathedral Basilica of the Assumption, Covington, Kentucky*. He serves as pastor of Holy Spirit Parish in Newport, Kentucky.

KIM DAVID

Kim David attended the University of Cincinnati and studied in the field of communications. She has been the driving force behind this book for the past 18 months. As a board member at The Summit Country Day School, Cincinnati, Ohio and having served in a variety of fundraising and leadership roles for non-profits, Mrs. David was naturally suited for her role as co-publisher of this book. Married with four daughters, she resides in Baltimore, Maryland with her husband Scott and is pursuing various ventures in the fields of publishing and e-commerce. Kim also enjoys coaching lacrosse and field hockey as well as wilderness ventures such as canoeing and camping. Her motto in life is, "if not now, when?"

ROBERT A. FLISCHEL

Robert A. Flischel graduated from Xavier University in 1971. He studied photography under Kazik Pazovski and credits his clean, direct style to Pazovski's influence. Mr. Flischel is a founding trustee of Radio Reading Service, which assists the visually impaired. He has served on the board of the regional chapter of The American Society of Media Photographers and is currently a Board Member and President Emeritus of The Art League of Cincinnati. This series of books on the cultural institutions of Cincinnati have been strongly influenced by the work of Ken Burns.

MARA MULVIHILL

Mara Mulvihill is a graduate of Walnut Hills High School and attended the University of Cincinnati. She was the Managing Editor for *The University of Cincinnati, Architectural Transformation: Tradition and Innovation*, RAF Press, 2007 and a Production Coordinator for *Cincinnati Illuminated, A Photographic Journey*, RAF Press, 2003. She is currently the Studio Manager for Robert

A. Flischel Photography and the Managing Editor for RAF Press.

MADISON DESIGN GROUP

Jackie Roberto and Julie Courtney, founders of Madison Design Group, became friends on their first day of drawing class at the University of Cincinnati's College of Design, Art, Architecture and Planning in 1985. Seven years after graduation, they formed Madison Design Group. Jonathan Albers, a College of Mount Saint Joseph graduate, was hired in 2001, and became partner in 2006. Madison Design Group specializes in external relations communications and design for Fortune 500 companies. We help those who are responsible for building and protecting corporate reputations communicate their brand identity to their stakeholders in ways that increase compliance, consistency and creativity.

A team of talented designers exhibited the company's trademark creativity, enthusiasm and commitment during this project. Jonathan Albers was a valuable resource with his project management and previous book experience. Tricia Bateman, Madison Design Group's Art Director, led the concept and creative direction of the book. Allison Leidy and Lindsey Meyer, both graduates of University of Cincinnati's College of Design, Art, Architecture and Planning, were responsible for bring this masterpiece to fruition.

JOE SIMON

Joe Simon has been a professional photographer since 1997. His first exhibit, a series of portraits of Tarahumara Indians from Copper Canyon in the Sierra Madre of Mexico, led him to a career exploring, with the same curiosity and intensity, other subjects: from landscapes and wildlife, to architecture and portraiture. Joe

is a regular contributor to *Xavier University Magazine*, *Cincinnati Enquirer*, *Catholic Telegraph*, and Food Network. Mr. Simon has collaborated on a variety of projects with Robert A. Flischel Photography over the past ten years. Joe lives with his wife Catalina in the Cincinnati neighborhood of Oakley. They have four children and four grandchildren.

MARGO WARMINSKI

A native of Detroit, Margo Warminski became interested in architecture and urbanism at an early age. She relocated to Cincinnati in 1977, drawn by the cities natural and man-made beauty. Margo earned a bachelor's degree in English from the University of Michigan in 1976 and studied urban planning and historic preservation at the University of Cincinnati. After spending many years as a historic preservation consultant in Cincinnati and Northern Kentucky, she became Preservation Director of Cincinnati Preservation Association in 2004. In addition to various research and writing projects, Margo is restoring a hundred-year-old house in Newport's East Row Historic District.

JAY YOCIS

Jay Yocis received his degree in fine arts from the University of Cincinnati in 1991. He has also been a photographer and videographer for his alma mater since the 1970s. His recent book, *Stories in Glass: The Windows of the Cathedral Basilica of the Assumption, Covington, Kentucky* by Monsignor William Cleves, was a stunning success. As a result of that book, he was contacted by RAF Press to become a contributing photographer for *Messages of Glory*. Jay's hope is that this book inspires people to visit these sacred spaces and become spiritually inspired by the beauty of the art they discover.

INDEX

COLOPHON

Messages of Glory was designed in 2011 by Madison Design Group of Covington, Ky. The design utilizes a grid based on the Gutenberg Bible and illuminated lettering inspired by the Book of Kells. The typeface used is Requiem, created by Jonathan Hoefler and Tobias Frere-Jones and inspired by Renaissance writing manuals.

St. Patrick, patron saint of Ireland. *Window by Franz Mayer of Munich, Germany. Formerly in Church of the Assumption, Walnut Hills, which was recently closed. It was removed, restored and reinstalled in St. Ignatius Loyola Church, Monford Heights, Oh.*